easy

Microsoft
Works Suite
2000

See it done

Do it yourself

que®

Part **3: Tracking Your Finances with Money 2000 Standard**

Easy Microsoft® Works Suite 2000
Copyright © 2000 by Que® Corporation

Library of Congress Catalog Card Number: 99-64716

International Standard Book Number: 0-7897-2217-8

Printed in the United States of America

First Printing: February, 2000

01 00 99   4 3 2 1

Trademarks

Warning and Disclaimer

Acknowledgments

I appreciate having the opportunity to join the great team at Que in producing this book. Acquisitions Editor Angelina Ward and Development Editor Sarah Robbins provided insight and expertise as they guided this project from start to finish. And editors Karen Shields, Victoria Elzey, and Maribeth Echard ensured the clarity and accuracy of the text in your hands. To these folks—along with the excellent designers, page layout experts, proofreaders, and sales and marketing staff—I extend my ongoing thanks, gratitude, and appreciation.

About the Author

An author and publishing consultant, **Lisa A. Bucki** has been involved in the computer books business for more than nine years. She wrote *PCs 6-in-1* (Que), *Easy Quicken 99* (Que), *Sams Teach Yourself Works Suite 99 in 24 Hours* (Sams), *Easy Microsoft Home Essentials 98* (Que), and many more. She also has written or contributed to a number of other books and multimedia products for Macmillan. Bucki now has more than 35 author and coauthor credits. Bucki has developed more than 100 computer and trade titles during her association with Macmillan. For Que Education and Training, Bucki created the Virtual Tutor CD-ROM companions for the *Essentials* series of books. Bucki recently wrote a response to a Request For Information (RFI) involving more than $300 million in business for a North Carolina–based manufacturing facility. Bucki also serves as a trainer (Word 97, Excel 97, and Project 98) for SofTrain, based in Asheville, N.C.

Publisher
Greg Wiegand

Acquisitions Editor
Angelina Ward

Development Editor
Sarah Robbins

Technical Editor
John Purdum

Managing Editor
Thomas F. Hayes

Project Editor
Karen S. Shields

Copy Editor
Victoria Elzey

Indexer
Kevin Kent

Proofreader
Maribeth Echard

Team Coordinator
Sharry Lee Gregory

Editorial Assistant
Angela Boley

Book Designer
Jean Bisesi

Cover Designer
Anne Jones

Production
Cynthia Davis-Hubler
Lisa England
Dan Harris
George Poole

How to Use This Book

It's as Easy as 1-2-3

Each part of this book is made up of a series of short, instructional lessons, designed to help you understand basic information that you need to get the most out of your computer hardware and software.

① Each step is fully illustrated to show you how it looks onscreen.

Click: Click the left mouse button once.

Double-click: Click the left mouse button twice in rapid succession.

① Tips and ① Warnings give you a heads-up for any extra information you may need while working through the task.

Right-click: Click the right mouse button once.

② Each task includes a series of quick, easy steps designed to guide you through the procedure.

Pointer Arrow: Highlights an item on the screen you need to point to or focus on in the step or task.

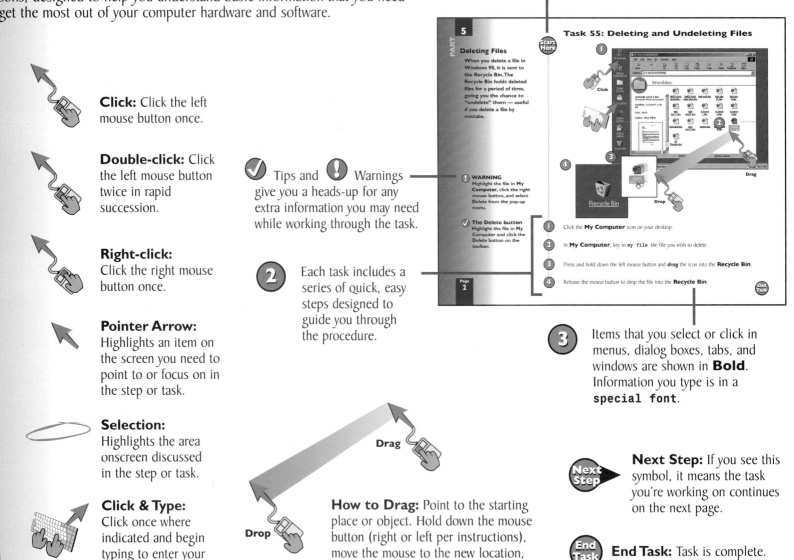

Selection: Highlights the area onscreen discussed in the step or task.

③ Items that you select or click in menus, dialog boxes, tabs, and windows are shown in Bold. Information you type is in a **special font**.

Click & Type: Click once where indicated and begin typing to enter your text or data.

Drag

Drop

How to Drag: Point to the starting place or object. Hold down the mouse button (right or left per instructions), move the mouse to the new location, and then release the button.

Next Step: If you see this symbol, it means the task you're working on continues on the next page.

End Task: Task is complete.

Introduction to Microsoft Works Suite 2000

Microsoft Home Works Suite offers several different Microsoft programs: Word 2000, Works and the Works Suite Task Launcher, Money 2000 Standard, Internet Explorer 5.0 and Outlook Express 5.0, the Address Book, Microsoft Home Publishing 2000, Picture It! Express, the Encarta 2000 Encyclopedia, and more.

This diverse collection of programs helps your computer serve as a resource for every family member who might need it to type a letter, double-check math calculations, or organize names and addresses. You can track your finances, or surf the Internet for entertainment or research. Save shopping time and money by creating personalized cards, stationery, and posters. You can even use the electronic encyclopedia to answer tricky questions or help you work through the crossword puzzle in your local paper. Works Suite 2000 contains *tasks* that guide you through the process of activities such as these:

- Create documents such as letters, lists, and certificates.

- Crunch numbers or keep an address book.

- Track your budget and write checks.

- Visit Web pages.

- Create your own greeting cards and other projects.

- Do research for a report.

With your home computer, Microsoft Works Suite 2000, and *Easy Microsoft Works Suite 2000* as your roadmap, you have everything you need to get started. You'll be creating documents and projects like a pro in no time!

Creating Documents with Word 2000

Word processing programs provide tools for creating text-oriented documents such as letters, memos, reports, flyers, newsletters, and so on. The Word 2000 skills you and your family members learn can come in handy in a variety of ways. This part shows you how to use Word 2000 to create a basic document, improve its appearance, and then print as many hard copies as you need.

Tasks

Starting and Exiting Word

After you start Word 2000, you can create your document text. When you finish working with Word, you use another command to exit the Word program. You also can launch Word from the Works Task Launcher (refer to Task 4 in Part 2).

✔ **Handling the Office Assistant**

Word 2000 also displays the Office Assistant help character the first time you start the program. To begin working, click the button beside **Start Using Microsoft Word**. If you're prompted to register Word, you can follow the onscreen directions to do so. To close the Office Assistant, right-click it and then click the **Hide** command.

Task 1: Starting and Exiting Word

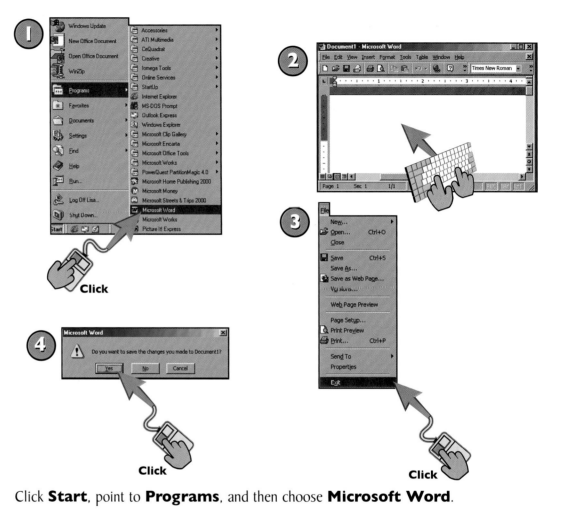

Click **Start**, point to **Programs**, and then choose **Microsoft Word**.

When Word 2000 opens onscreen, you can type and format your text.

Choose **File**, **Exit** or press **Alt+F4** when you're ready to exit Word.

If prompted, click **Yes** to save your changes (see Task 23, "Closing a Document File," for more about saving) or **No** to exit.

End Task

Task 2: Typing Text in a Document

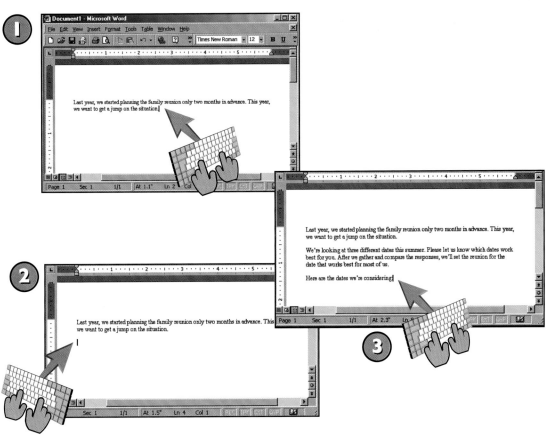

Start Here

Entering Text

In Word 2000, each keyboard character you press appears at the blinking vertical *insertion point*, which moves to the right as you type. When the text fills the line, the *word wrap* feature automatically moves the insertion point to the next line. Pressing **Enter** starts a new paragraph (called a *paragraph break*). When you fill a page, Word 2000 automatically inserts a *soft page break* (an automatic page break) to start a new page for you.

(1) Type your first paragraph, letting text at the right margin wrap to the next line as needed.

(2) Press **Enter** to start a new paragraph and press **Enter** again, if needed, to insert a blank line.

(3) Repeat steps 1 and 2 to add additional paragraphs.

✓ Click and Type
You can enter text anywhere on the page rather. **Double-click to position the insertion point** where you'd like the text to appear, and then start typing. Word adjusts the way text lines up depending on where you enter it.

End Task

Task 3: Moving the Insertion Point

Moving the Insertion Point

Whatever you type in Word appears at the location of the flashing vertical insertion point. So, it follows that when you want to make changes, you need to move the insertion point to the location of the text to change. After you've moved the insertion point to the correct location, you can use the techniques covered in Task 4, "Making Simple Changes," to edit the text. Moving the insertion point automatically *scrolls* the onscreen text, so you can see what you're editing.

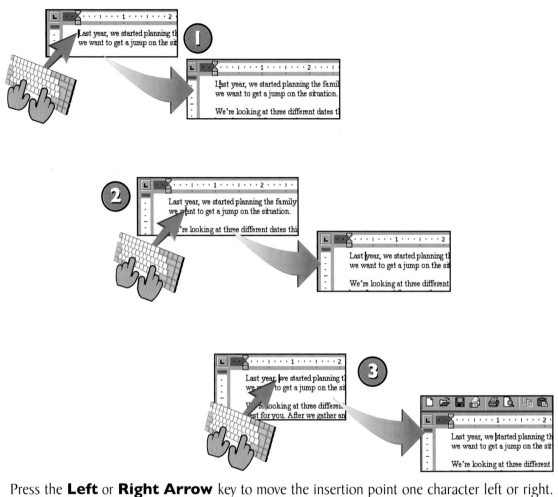

✓ **Click Your Spot**
You can click with the mouse to move the insertion point. The I-beam mouse pointer appears when you hover the mouse over text. When the I-beam reaches the position you want for the insertion point, click the mouse.

1 Press the **Left** or **Right Arrow** key to move the insertion point one character left or right.

2 Press the **Up** or **Down Arrow** key to move the insertion point one line up or down.

3 Press **Ctrl+Left Arrow** or **Ctrl+Right Arrow** to move the insertion point one word left or right.

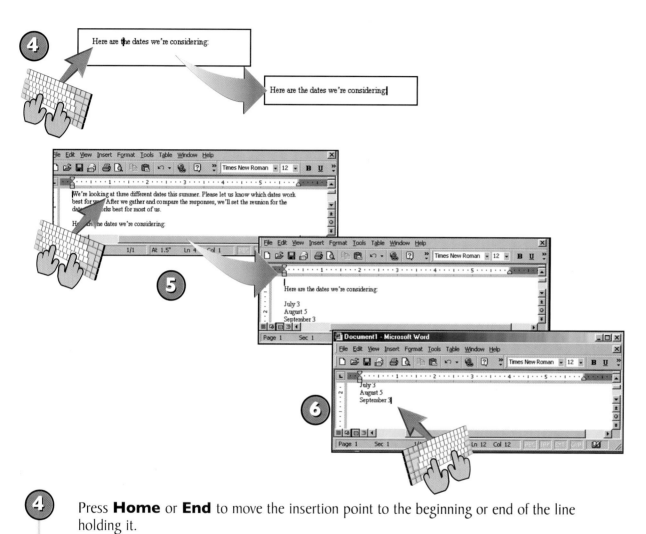

Using the Scrollbar

You can use the vertical scrollbar at the right side of the document to display other areas. Drag the scrollbar box up or down until you see the page number for the page you want to display and then release the mouse button, or click the up or down arrow on the bar to scroll in either direction. You also can click the **Previous Page** or **Next Page** buttons (each has a double-arrow) at the bottom of the scrollbar to display the previous or next page.

⚠ WARNING

Keep in mind that scrolling the document does not move the insertion point. After you use the vertical scrollbar or the Previous Page or Next Page buttons to scroll the document, click to position the insertion point in the onscreen text.

(4) Press **Home** or **End** to move the insertion point to the beginning or end of the line holding it.

(5) Press **PgUp** or **PgDn** to move the insertion point up or down by one screenful of information.

(6) Press **Ctrl+Home** or **Ctrl+End** to move the insertion point to the beginning or end of the document.

Making Changes to Text

Even though word processors like Word 2000 offer a host of fancy features, you can do most of your editing work using a few simple techniques. You can use the keyboard to make many changes to your text, either as you're typing or at a later time when you're working with the document. For most users, the keyboard remains the primary editing tool because you can make your changes without lifting a hand to work with the mouse.

Working with a Text Block

You can select a block of text and then delete, replace, move, or copy the whole thing. Tasks 5 through 9 cover these techniques.

Task 4: Making Simple Changes

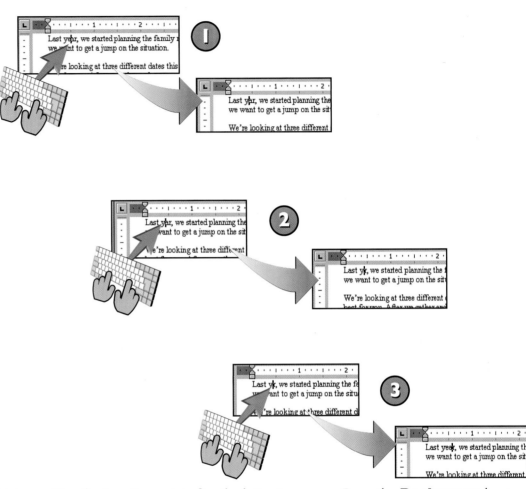

① Click to position the insertion point after the letter to remove. Press the **Backspace** key to remove the character to the left of the insertion point.

② Press the **Delete** key to remove the character to the right of the insertion point.

③ Type new text to add it to the left of the insertion point.

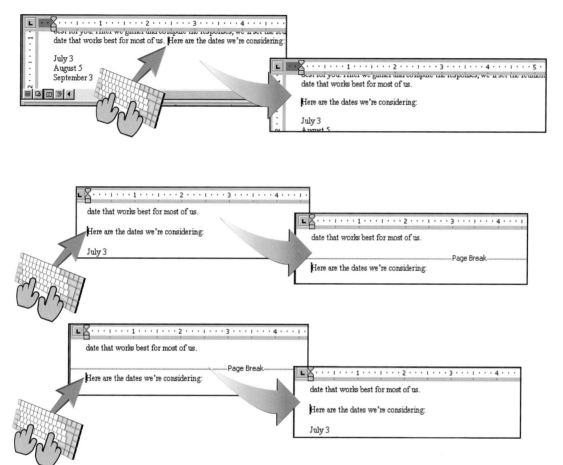

Controlling Page Breaks

If you add or remove a large amount of text in a document, Word 2000 automatically inserts and removes soft (automatic) page breaks. You can force or insert a *hard page break* (also called a *manual page break*) where you need it, as described in step 5.

✔ **Tabbing Over**
Press **Tab** to move the insertion point to the next *tab stop* (preset alignment measurement), so that you can type text starting at the tab stop. Word has a tab stop set every 0.5".

✔ **Viewing Page Breaks**
The appearance of page break varies depending on which document *view* you're using. Steps 5 and 6 show the page break in the Normal view. Task 28, "Changing Between Print Layout and Normal Views," explains how to change views.

④ Press **Enter** once (or twice to insert a blank line) to start a new paragraph at the insertion point.

⑤ Click to position the insertion point where you want to start a new page, and then press **Ctrl+Enter**.

⑥ Click after a page or paragraph break or blank line, and then press **Backspace** to delete it.

Selecting Text

Rather than working a word or character at a time, you can *select* a larger amount of text so that actions you perform—including editing and formatting actions—are applied to the entire selection. Word 2000 offers a number of different mouse and keyboard techniques for selecting text. Because black reverse highlighting appears over the selected text, you might also hear folks use the words *highlighting text* to describe making a selection.

 WARNING

Be careful when you select text. If you accidentally press a key while you have a selection highlighted, you could obliterate the whole selection. Immediately press **Ctrl+Z** to get it back.

Task 5: Selecting Text

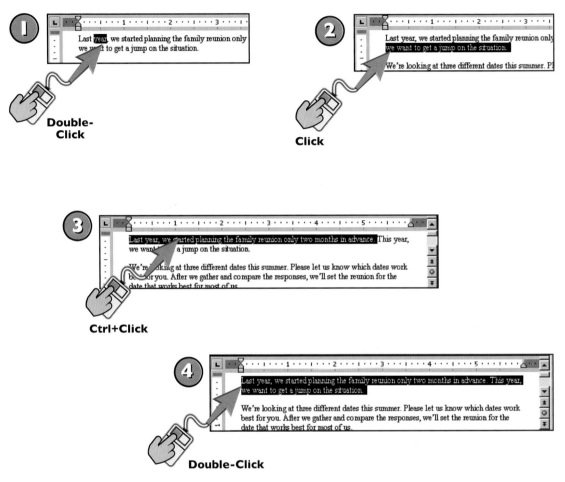

Start Here

① **Double-Click**

② **Click**

③ **Ctrl+Click**

④ **Double-Click**

① Double-click any word to select it.

② Click in the left margin next to a line to select the entire line. (The mouse pointer should become a right-slanting arrow before you click.)

③ Press and hold **Ctrl** and click a sentence to select the whole sentence.

④ Double-click in the left margin next to a paragraph to select the whole paragraph.

Next Step

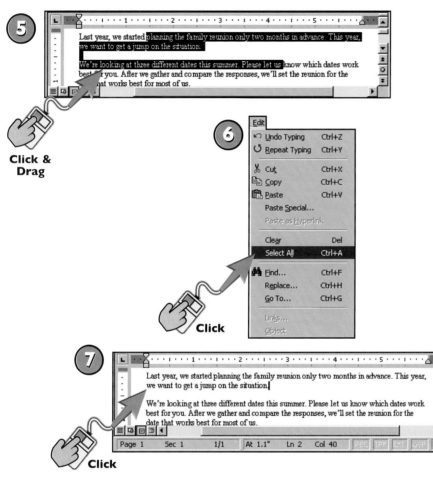

**Selecting an
Irregular Area**

To choose an irregular
selection, you also can click
at the beginning of the
block, scroll to display the
end of the block to select,
press and hold **Shift**, and
then click at the end of the
block. This technique works
better if you find that your
screen scrolls too quickly
when you try to make a
selection by dragging alone.

5 Drag over an irregular block of text to select it.

6 Choose **Edit**, **Select All** to select all the document text.

7 To cancel a selection, click outside the selection in another area of the document.

**Selecting with the
Keyboard**
To use the keyboard alone to
make a selection, press and hold
Shift, and then press any arrow
key to extend the selection. Or,
press and hold **Shift+Ctrl**, and
then press the **Up** or **Down
Arrow** to extend the selection
by a paragraph at a time.

Deleting and Replacing Text

You can use a few different techniques to correct text in a document more quickly. For starters, you can delete a whole selection—even all the text in the document if you've selected all of it. By default, Word works in *Insert mode*, meaning that text you type appears at the insertion point, and existing text moves further right. To replace the text to the right instead of moving it, you can turn on *Overtype Mode* and type the replacement information.

But It Was a Mistake!
If you make a mistake while deleting or replacing text, you can undo it. See Task 10, "Undoing and Redoing a Change," to learn how to fix mistakes.

Task 6: Deleting and Replacing Text

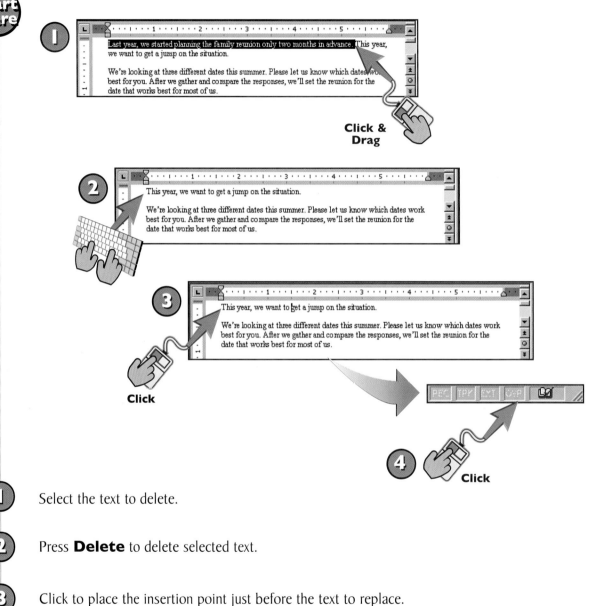

1. Select the text to delete.

2. Press **Delete** to delete selected text.

3. Click to place the insertion point just before the text to replace.

4. Double-click the **OVR** indicator on the status bar or press **Insert** to turn on Overtype mode.

Next Step

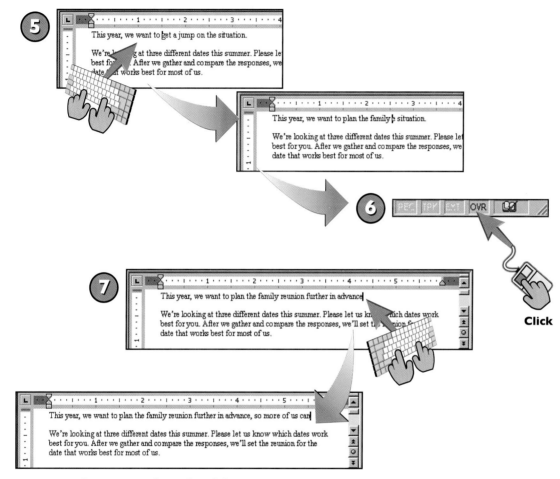

Avoiding Overtype Mistakes

When you're working in Overtype mode, be sure to watch how much you type. As long as Overtype mode is active, your typing replaces text to the right of the insertion point. You don't want to type over information that you need to keep, which is easy to do in Overtype mode.

Click

5 Type to replace text to the right of the insertion point in overtype mode.

6 Double-click the **OVR** indicator on the status bar or press **Insert** to return to Insert mode.

7 Type to insert new text at the insertion point location.

⚠ **WARNING**
If you have some text selected when typing in either Insert mode or Overtype mode, the first key you press will replace the entire selection. If you don't want to replace the selection, click to move the insertion point before you type.

Moving Text

When you move information in Windows applications, you remove it from its current location and insert it into its new location. *Cutting* a selection removes it from the document and places it in the *Clipboard*, which serves as a holding area for cut information until you *paste* the information to insert it at its new location. You can cut and paste information to move it quicker than you can delete and retype it.

(!) WARNING
Double-check the area from which you cut the text and the area to which you pasted it to see whether you need to insert or delete any extra spaces. Also press **Enter** to begin a new paragraph where needed.

(!) WARNING
Pressing the **Delete** or **Backspace** key to remove a selection does not place the selection on the Clipboard.

Task 7: Moving Text

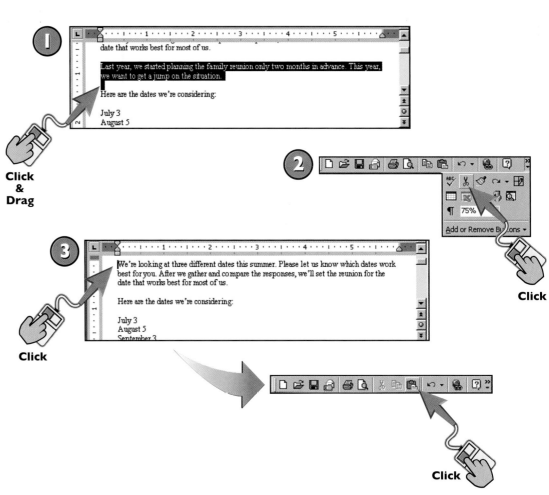

Click & Drag

Click

Click

Click

1. Select the text to move.

2. Click the **More Buttons** button on the Standard toolbar, and then click the **Cut** button to move the selection from the document to the Clipboard.

3. Click to place the insertion point where you want to insert the cut text.

4. Click the **Paste** button to past the text at its new location.

Task 8: Copying Text

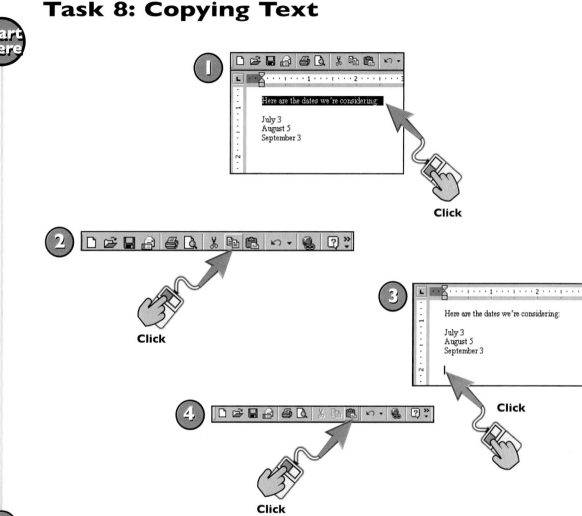

Start Here

Click

Click

Click

Click

Copying Text

Copying a selection duplicates it and places the copy in the *Clipboard*. It remains in the Clipboard holding area until you *paste* the copied information to insert it at a new location.

✓ **Pop-Up Clipboard**
If you perform Task 8 immediately after Task 7, the Clipboard toolbar might open. Task 9 explains how to use that toolbar. Click the **Close (X)** button on the toolbar to close it. Also notice that because you used the Cut button in Task 7, it now appears on the Standard toolbar. Word's *personalized menus and toolbars* feature updates menus and toolbars with commands and buttons you use often.

1 Select the text to copy.

2 Click the **Copy** button to duplicate the selection in the document and place the copy on the Clipboard.

3 Click to place the insertion point where you want to insert the copy of the text.

4 Click the **Paste** button to past the text at its new location.

✓ **More Space, Please**
When you move or copy text to the very end of the document, you might need to press **Enter** once to insert a blank line to hold the pasted text.

End Task

Understanding the Office Clipboard

In addition to being part of Works Suite, Word 2000 plays a key role in the Office 2000 Suite from Microsoft. Office 2000 and its applications provide an enhancement to the standard Windows clipboard called the *Office Clipboard*. While the Windows clipboard can hold only one copied or cut selection until you copy or cut again, the Office Clipboard holds up to 12 selections that you cut or copy. This means you can make edits—pasting text and other items you've cut or copied into the proper position—in the order that you prefer.

✓ **Paste It Again**

After you cut or copy information to the Office Clipboard, you can paste it into multiple locations.

Task 9: Using the New Office Clipboard

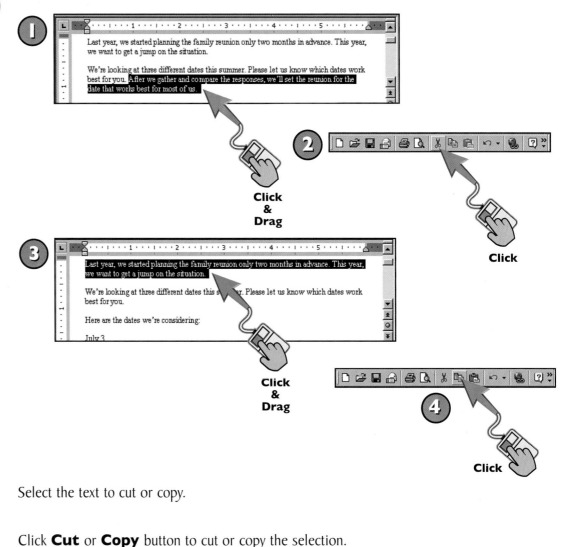

Click & Drag

Click

Click & Drag

Click

① Select the text to cut or copy.

② Click **Cut** or **Copy** button to cut or copy the selection.

③ Make another selection to cut or copy.

④ Click the **Cut** or **Copy** button to cut or copy the selection. The Office Clipboard appears.

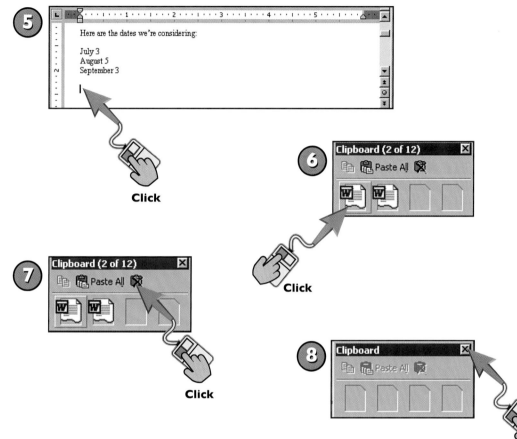

Displaying and Hiding the Office Clipboard Toolbar

The Office Clipboard appears in Word as the Clipboard toolbar. When you want to close the Clipboard toolbar, click its **Close (X)** button. Closing the Clipboard toolbar does not clear the Clipboard toolbar contents, so you can redisplay the Clipboard toolbar at any time to paste items from it. To redisplay the Clipboard toolbar, right-click on any toolbar, and then click **Clipboard** in the shortcut menu that appears.

✓ **Fill 'Er Up**
If you try to place a 13th item on the Office Clipboard, Word asks whether you want to throw away the first item on the Clipboard to make room for the new one. If you click **OK**, the next item you cut or copy replaces the first item.

Click

Click

Click

Click

⑤ Click to place the insertion point where you want to insert a selection from the Office Clipboard.

⑥ Click on the Clipboard item you'd like to insert.

⑦ Click the **Clear Clipboard** button to clear the contents of the Clipboard toolbar.

⑧ Click the **Close (X)** button to close the Office Clipboard (Clipboard toolbar).

Task 10: Undoing and Redoing a Change

Using Undo and Redo

If you make a mistake while working with text, use the *undo* feature to cancel the change and reinstate the text to its prior state. You can undo either the change you just made or several recent changes. Word 2000 keeps a list of your changes. When you choose a change to undo from this list, Word undoes that change, plus all changes above it in the list. If you undo a change but decide to reinstate it, you can use *redo*. If you undid several actions, they appear in a list, and you can redo one or more of them.

✓ **Undo and Redo Keyboard Shortcuts**
Press **Ctrl+Z** to undo the last change you made and **Ctrl+Y** to redo it.

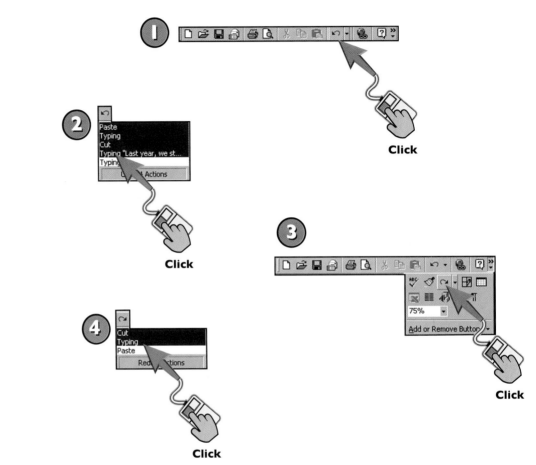

Start Here

Click

Click

Click

Click

1. Click the **Undo** button to undo your most recent change.

2. Click the **Undo** drop-down arrow, and then click an action or change to undo it and the changes above it.

3. Click the **Redo** button (click the **More Buttons** button first, if needed) to redo your most recent change.

4. Click the **Redo** drop-down arrow, and then click a change to redo it and the changes above it.

End Task

Task 11: Making a Change with Drag and Drop

Start Here

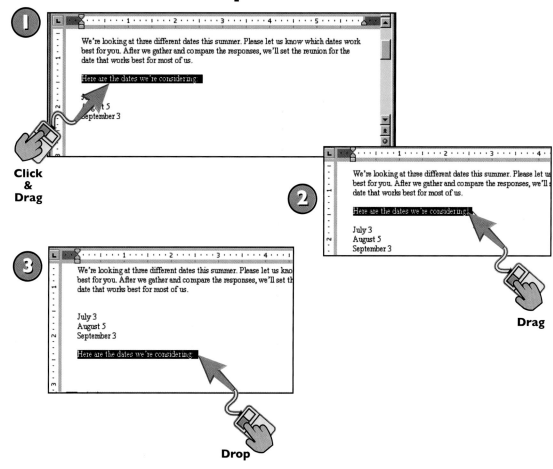

Click & Drag

Drag

Drop

Using Drag and Drop

To move text a short distance, simply drag it from one location to another with *drag and drop* editing. After you become comfortable with the mouse, you'll use a combination of keyboard techniques, toolbar buttons, and drag and drop to make changes in your document.

WARNING

Although you can drag and drop information as far as you want in a document, it's a little tough to control document scrolling while you drag and drop. So, use drag and drop to make a change within a sentence or paragraph, and use cut and paste for moves between different pages.

Drag and Drop a Copy

Press and hold the **Ctrl** key before you press the left mouse button. Hold down the **Ctrl** key while you drag. When you release the mouse button to drop the text, Word inserts a copy of the original selection.

① Select the text to move.

② Press and hold the left mouse button and drag the text. A box appears beside the mouse pointer as you drag.

③ Release the mouse button to drop the text into place.

Adding or Removing Text Formatting

When you change the appearance of a word, paragraph, or page, you're changing its *formatting*. Many beginners start out making modest format changes—say, applying **boldface**, *italic*, or <u>underlining</u> to a few words for emphasis. You might see boldface, italic, and underlining called "attributes."

✓ Finding the Formatting Toolbar

Use the buttons on the Formatting toolbar to apply formatting changes to text. **By default, the Formatting toolbar appears to the right of the Standard toolbar. The** Bold, Italic, and Underline buttons described in this task appear on the Formatting toolbar.

Task 12: Adding or Removing Boldface, Italic, or Underlining

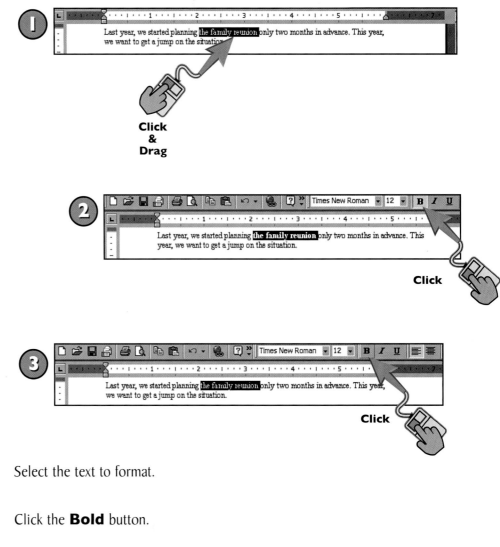

Start Here

Click & Drag

Click

Click

1. Select the text to format.

2. Click the **Bold** button.

3. Click the **Bold** button again to remove the boldface.

Next Step

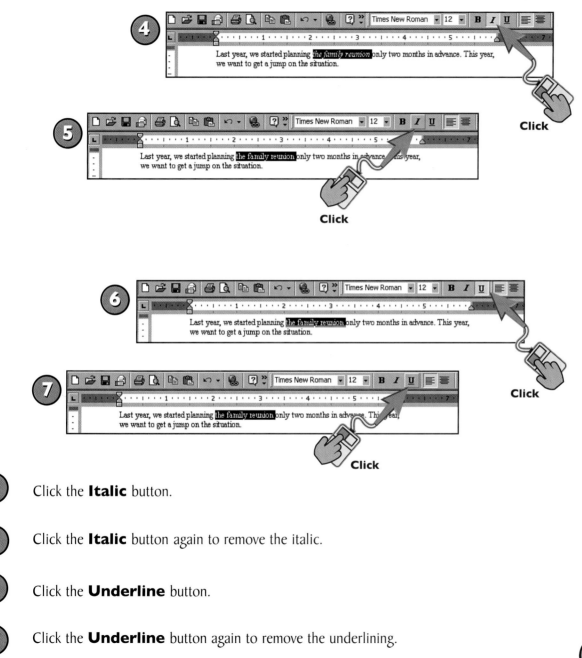

Applying Attributes As You Type

You can turn boldface, italic, or underlining on to apply them to text as you type. Click the toolbar button(s) for the attribute(s) to turn on, type the text, and click the button(s) again to turn the attribute off. You can press **Ctrl+B** to apply or remove boldface, **Ctrl+I** for italic, and **Ctrl+U** for underlining.

✅ Removing an Attribute

When you apply an attribute to a selection, the Bold, Italic, or Underline button looks "pushed" or indented, indicating the attribute is active to the selection. Click the button to remove the attribute and pop the button back up.

✅ Clearing Attributes

If you want to remove multiple attributes from a selection simultaneously, press **Ctrl+Spacebar**.

④ Click the **Italic** button.

⑤ Click the **Italic** button again to remove the italic.

⑥ Click the **Underline** button.

⑦ Click the **Underline** button again to remove the underlining.

End Task

Task 13: Choosing Another Font (Look) for Text

Changing Font

The *font* determines the distinctive shape and weight of characters. You can apply any font that's installed in Windows to a selection in a Word document.

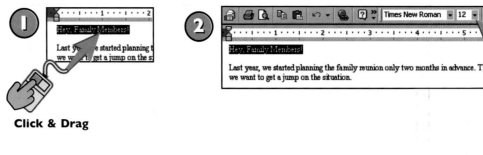

Click & Drag

Click

✅ Using the Font Dialog Box

If you want to change numerous different formatting selections at once—such as the font, attributes, and more— choose **Format, Font.** Change the settings you want on the Font tab in the Font dialog box. The Preview area shows how the current settings look. Click **OK** to finish changing the settings.

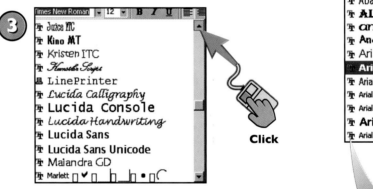

Click

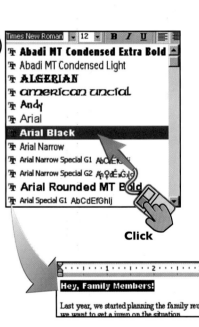

Click

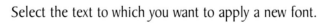

⚠ WARNING

Using too many fonts in a single document makes it look like a ransom note. Generally, stick with one font for headings (titles), another for body text, and perhaps a third to accent selected areas.

1 Select the text to which you want to apply a new font.

2 Click the **Font** drop-down list arrow on the Formatting toolbar.

3 Use the scroll arrows on the list to display the font you want.

4 Click the font you want to apply to the selection.

End Task

Task 14: Choosing Another Size for Text

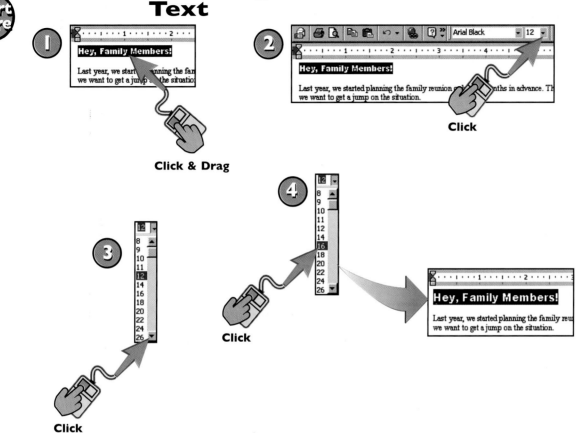

Click & Drag

Click

Click

Click

Changing Text Size

You can make text larger to make it more readable or smaller to fit more on a page. Windows applications measure text size in *points*, with each point equal to 1/72 of an inch.

---

① Select the text to which you want to apply a new font size.

② Click the **Font Size** drop-down list arrow on the Formatting toolbar.

③ Use the scroll arrows on the list to display the size you want.

④ Click the size you want to apply to the selection.

✓ **Entering a Font Size**
Rather than opening and scrolling the Font Size list, you can click in the Font Size text box on the Formatting toolbar, type the size you want (in points), and press **Enter**.

Task 15: Applying a Color to Text

Coloring Text

You can change the color of a text selection to help that text stand out. Use a limited number of colors to ensure the document remains readable and attractive. You'll achieve the best results if you apply color only to headings or titles, and words you want to emphasize.

(!) WARNING

Light colors are hard to read onscreen or on white paper, so choose easy-to-read bold colors, instead. Otherwise, let your printer's capabilities dictate your color choices. Black-and-white printers convert colors to shades of gray, so choose colors that contrast well.

(✓) Keep On Coloring

After you choose a color from the Font Color palette, the color remains active and the Font Color button remains on the toolbar. Click the Font Color button to apply the color to other selections.

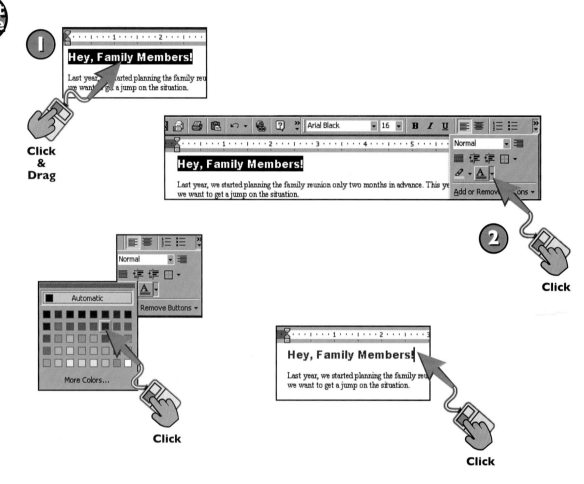

Start Here

Click & Drag

Click

Click

Click

Click

(1) Select the text to which you want to apply a new color.

(2) Click the **More Buttons** button at the right end of the Formatting toolbar, and then click the **Font Color** drop-down list arrow.

(3) Click the color you want in the palette to select it and apply it to the selection.

(4) Click outside the selection to see the color.

End Task

Task 16: Choosing How Text Lines Up

Start Here

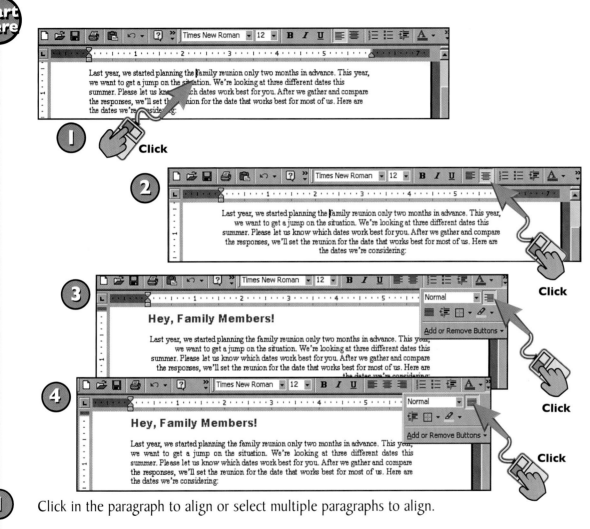

Click

Aligning Text

Every printed page has blank space around the edges called the *margin*. You can control how each paragraph of text aligns relative to the left and right margins. **Align Left** lines up each line in a paragraph along the left margin, and is the default setting. **Center** positions each line of text in the paragraph equidistant between the margins. **Align Right** pushes each line of text in the paragraph against the right margin. **Justify** adds spacing within each line so that both sides of the paragraph line up to the margin.

1. Click in the paragraph to align or select multiple paragraphs to align.

2. Click the **Center** button on the Formatting toolbar to center the text.

3. Click **More Buttons** button on the Formatting toolbar, and then click the **Align Right** button to right-align the text.

4. Click the **More Buttons** button on the Formatting toolbar, and then click the **Justify** button to justify the text.

✓ **Back Left**
Click the **Align Left** button to return to the default Align Left setting.

End Task

Task 17: Changing Spacing Between Lines

Changing Line Spacing

By default, Word uses single-line spacing in the paragraphs you type. That is, each line is about the same height as the font size, with a bit of spacing thrown in to accommodate capital letters and make text readable. You can select one or more paragraphs in the document and change the line spacing, increasing the spacing to 1.5 lines or double-spacing.

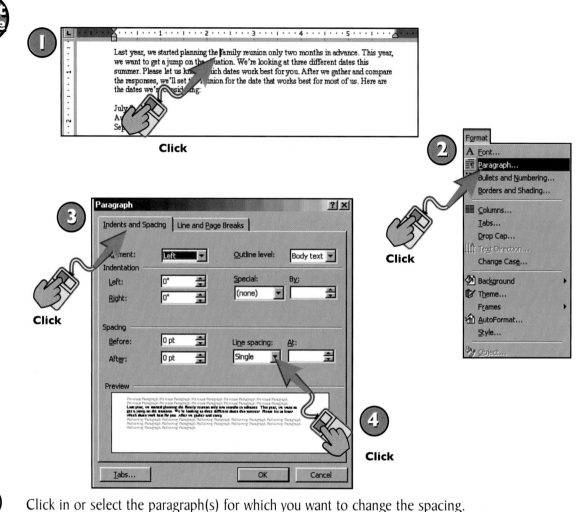

Start Here

Click

Click

Click

Click

(!) **WARNING**

If you press Enter an extra time between paragraphs to insert a blank line and then apply double spacing, keep in mind that you'll end up with four lines' worth of space between paragraphs.

(1) Click in or select the paragraph(s) for which you want to change the spacing.

(2) Choose **Format**, **Paragraph**.

(3) Click the **Indents and Spacing** tab.

(4) Click the **Line Spacing** drop-down list arrow.

Next Step

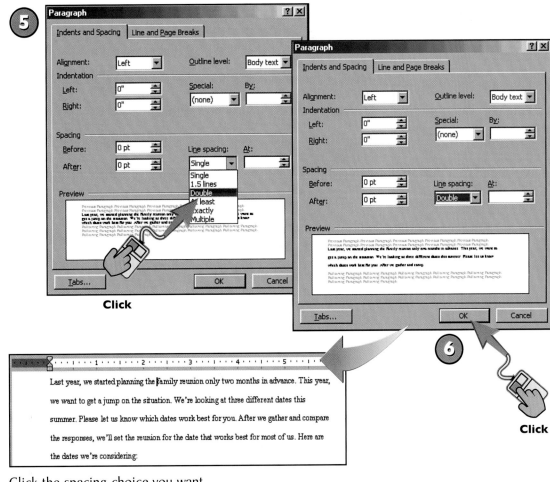

Click

Click

Fine-Tuning Paragraph Spacing

Rather than press **Enter**, you can insert a precise amount of extra space before or after a paragraph. To do so, enter the desired amount of spacing, in points, in the **Before** or **After** text box of the Indents and Spacing tab in the Paragraph dialog box.

Last year, we started planning the family reunion only two months in advance. This year, we want to get a jump on the situation. We're looking at three different dates this summer. Please let us know which dates work best for you. After we gather and compare the responses, we'll set the reunion for the date that works best for most of us. Here are the dates we're considering:

5 Click the spacing choice you want.

6 Click **OK** to close the dialog box and apply the spacing.

✓ **Spacing for Headings**
Graphic designers often add a bit of extra spacing before heading paragraphs, to set them off from preceding text.

Adding and Removing Bullets and Numbers

You can create attractive numbered or bulleted lists with a mouse click or two. Applying numbers or bullets not only inserts the number or bullet, but also properly indents each item in the list for a neat appearance. Word numbers or bullets each paragraph in the selection to which you add bullets or numbers. To insert additional items within the list, press **Enter**. Word creates the new list item (paragraph).

✓ **Missing Buttons?**
The **Numbering** and **Bullets** buttons appear on the Formatting toolbar by default, but might become hidden as you use other toolbar buttons. Use the **More Buttons** button on any toolbar to find a button that you need to use.

Task 18: Adding and Removing Bullets and Numbers

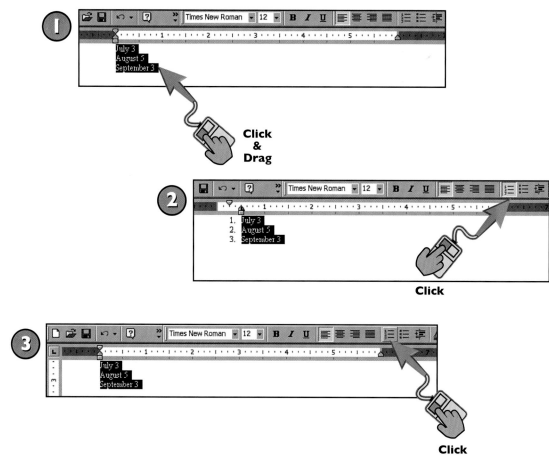

Start Here

Click & Drag

Click

Click

(1) Select the paragraph(s) to which you want to apply numbers or bullets.

(2) Click the **Numbering** button on the Formatting toolbar to apply numbering.

(3) Click the **Numbering** button to remove numbering from a selection.

Next Step

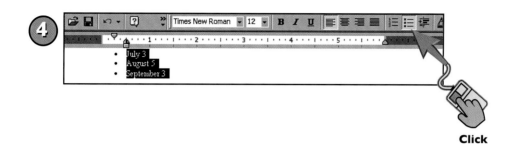

Click

Turning Off Bullets or Numbers

If you press **Enter** at the end of a bulleted or numbered paragraph to create a new paragraph, Word assigns a bullet or number to the new paragraph, too. To stop the bulleting or numbering, click the **Numbering** or **Bullets** button to turn off that feature.

Click

4 Click the **Bullets** button on the Formatting toolbar to apply bullets.

5 Click the **Bullets** button to remove bullets from a selection.

Inserting Clip Art

Word 2000 includes a number of predrawn pictures, called *Clip Art*, that you can insert into a document. Even if you're not an artistic genius or don't have access to images from another source, you can add attractive, colorful images to any document. The Microsoft Clip Gallery divides the Clip Art into categories, such as Animals, Entertainment, and Household. First, choose the category to see the pictures it holds and choose the picture to insert into the document.

 Even More Clips

After you open the Clip Gallery (the Insert ClipArt window), you can use its **Import Clips** button to add clips from another disk location into the Gallery. Or, use the **Clips Online** button to download more art from a **Microsoft Web** site with clips.

Task 19: Inserting a Clip Art Picture

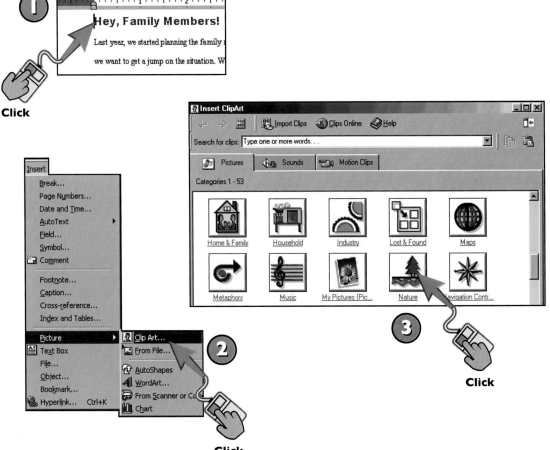

Start Here

Click

Click

Click

(1) Click to position the insertion point at the approximate location where you want to place the Clip Art.

(2) Choose **Insert**, **Picture**, **Clip Art**.

(3) Scroll down the Pictures tab, if needed, and then click the icon for the desired clip art category.

Next Step

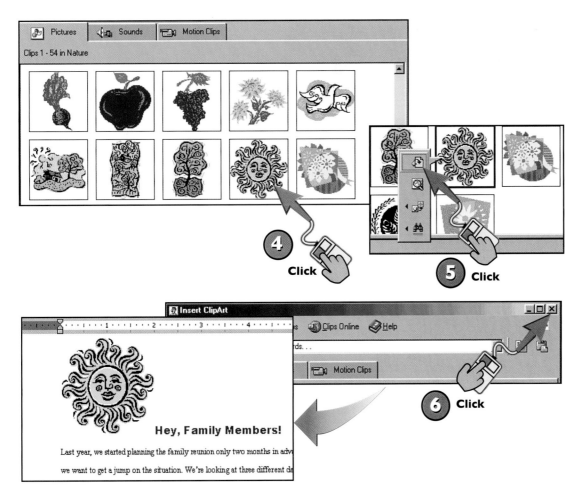

Working with Clip Art

In Word 2000, you can see clip art that you've inserted in any view. to work with a clip art image, click it to select it. Black handles and a Picture toolbar appear. Press **Delete** to delete the clip art, or drag a handle to resize it. Or, use one of the buttons on the Picture toolbar to make changes to it. When you finish, click outside the clip art image to deselect it.

Click

Click

Click

Hey, Family Members!

Last year, we started planning the family reunion only two months in adv we want to get a jump on the situation. We're looking at three different de

4 Scroll the image preview area and click the clip art image you want to insert.

5 Click the **Insert Clip** button at the top of the pop-up that appears.

6 Click the **Close (X)** button for the Insert ClipArt window to see the inserted clip art.

WARNING
If you try to insert a piece of clip art and see a message that it's missing and should be found in a folder on a disc inserted into your **CD-ROM** drive, click **Cancel**, insert Disc I of the Works Suite 2000 setup discs, and then after a few moments try again to insert the clip art.

End Task

Task 20: Creating WordArt

Creating WordArt

If you want to call attention to a phrase or headline in a document—I mean really make it stand out—mere color and font changes won't do the job. Instead, you can create *WordArt*, which enables you to choose a special effect look for text you enter. Your WordArt text can be curved, 3D, shadowed, or all three together.

Start Here

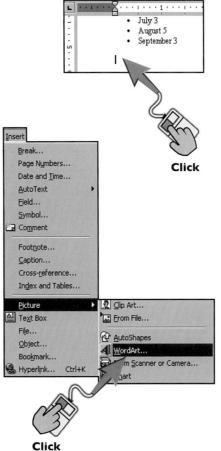

Click

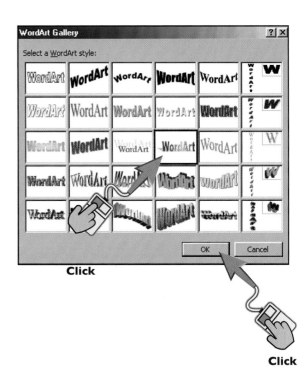

Click

Click

Click

(!) **WARNING**

Use clip art and WordArt sparingly. Although no one wants to rain on your creativity, too much artwork might not only distract your reader, but also make your files very large. In fact, you could make a file so large that it wouldn't fit on a floppy disk—a problem if you need to take the file to work or copy it to another computer.

1 Click to position the insertion point at the approximate location where you want to create the WordArt.

2 Choose **Insert**, **Picture**, **WordArt**.

3 In the WordArt Gallery dialog box, click the WordArt look you want, and then click **OK**.

Next Step

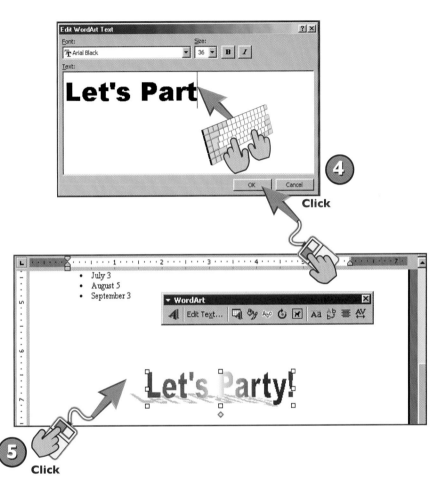

Designing Your WordArt

WordArt works best for short, snappy statements. If you try to cram too much into a WordArt object, it might not be readable. Plus, WordArt objects can be large and leave little room for regular text in your document. You can use the buttons on the WordArt toolbar to change the formatting for the WordArt object to make it more readable or attractive.

4 Type the WordArt text, and then click **OK**.

5 Click outside the WordArt image to deselect it and hide the WordArt toolbar.

✅ Formatting WordArt Text

Before you type your WordArt text, you can use the Font and Size drop-down lists and the Bold and Italic buttons to adjust the look of the text.

Checking Spelling and Grammar

With typewriters, spelling and grammar errors were difficult to correct. In a word processor, you can easily make changes before you print. Word can check your spelling and grammar for you, and help you make needed corrections.

⓵ WARNING

The spelling and grammar check capabilities in Word can save you a lot of time and embarrassment. However, you should not rely on them alone to make your documents accurate. Checking spelling and grammar doesn't catch certain types of mistakes, such as if you tell someone to "turn north" instead of "turn south" in a memo giving directions to a meeting location or if you confuse similar words such as "there" and "their." Always proofread your documents for accuracy.

Task 21: Checking Your Spelling and Grammar

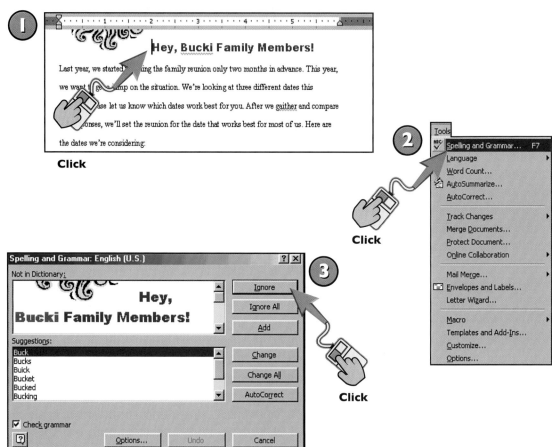

Click to position the insertion point at the beginning of the text to check.

Choose **Tools**, **Spelling and Grammar**.

If the word(s) highlighted in the Not in Dictionary list does not need correction, click **Ignore**.

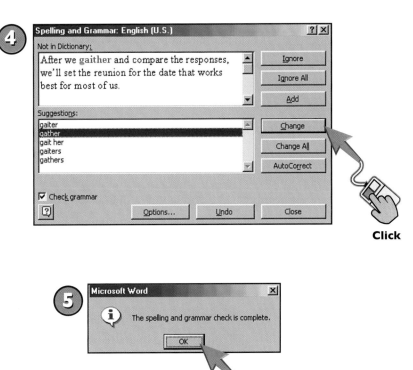

Click

Click

Making Faster Corrections

If you see a wavy red underline below a word, that means that Word thinks it might be misspelled. A wavy green underline under a phrase means that there might be a grammar error in the underlined text. Right-click the underlined word or phrase, and click the correct spelling or grammar change in the shortcut menu that appears. Word then corrects the word or phrase.

④ If the word(s) highlighted in the Not in Dictionary list needs to be changed, click the correct suggestion in the Suggestions list, and then click **Change**.

⑤ After you repeat steps 4 and 5 to correct all the spelling and grammar mistakes, click **OK** to conclude the check.

✅ **Checking on Command**

You can use the Spelling and Grammar button on the Standard toolbar (use the More Buttons button if you don't see it) or press F7 to run a spell check. To check a single word, select it before running the check.

Saving and Naming a File

You need to save your document file to give it a name and store the file on a hard disk. You can save your Word files in the default disk and folder c:\My Documents\, or another disk or folder of your choosing. Your filenames can be very descriptive because they can include more than 200 characters, spaces, and special capitalization.

✓ **Save Reminders**
If you forget to save your changes and try to exit Word, Word reminds you to save the file.

✓ **Up to a Higher Folder**
If you're viewing the contents of a folder within a disk and want to back up to see the list of all the folders in the disk, click the **Up One Level** button (it has a folder with an arrow) on the dialog box's toolbar. This is called "moving up a level in the folder tree."

Task 22: Saving and Naming Your Document File

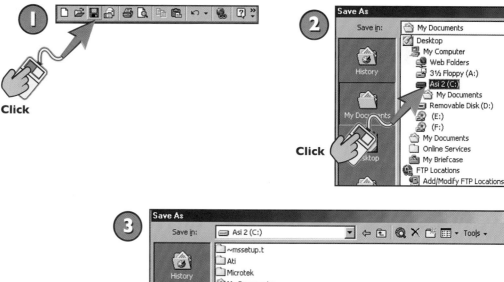

Click

Click

① Click the **Save** button on the Standard toolbar.

② To save to a disk or folder other than the default one, click it in the **Save In** list.

③ If the disk or folder you selected contains other folders, double-click the one to save to in the list.

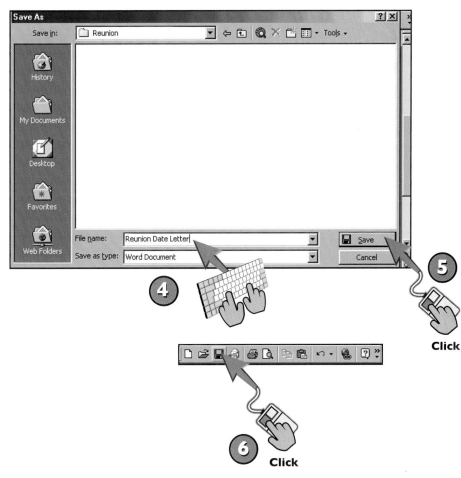

Saving a File with a New Name

After you save a file, you can choose **File, Save As** to redisplay the Save As dialog box. If you enter a new **File Name** and then click **Save**, Word saves a copy of the file under the new name. (To save to another folder, use the Save In list to select it before clicking Save.)

✓ **Save As You Go**
You should save your file every 10 minutes or so. This helps ensure that you won't lose as much work if your system reboots due to power fluctuations or crashes.

✓ **Going Places**
The Save As and Open dialog boxes in Word include the *Places Bar* at the left side. Click on the **My Documents** button there to go back to c:\My Documents\. Click the **History** button to see a list of shortcuts to files and folders you've worked with recently.

Click

Click

④ Drag over and then edit the suggested filename in the **File Name** text box.

⑤ Click the **Save** button.

⑥ To resave the file after you've saved it the first time, click the **Save** button on the Standard toolbar.

Task 23: Closing a Document File

Closing a File

When you finish working with a file, you should close it to remove it from your computer's memory. Closing also prevents you from making unwanted changes to the document.

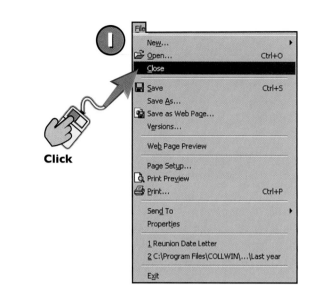

Click

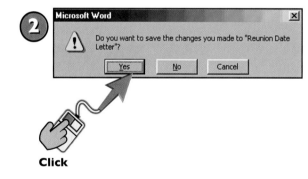

Click

Full Menus

If you want to display full menus in Word 2000, like those shown in this book, choose **Tools, Customize**. Click the **Options** tab, and then click to clear the check beside **Menus Show Recently Used Commands First**. Click **Close** to apply your change.

1 Choose **File**, **Close**.

2 If the file contains changes you haven't saved, click **Yes** to save your changes.

Task 24: Creating a New, Blank Document

Start Here

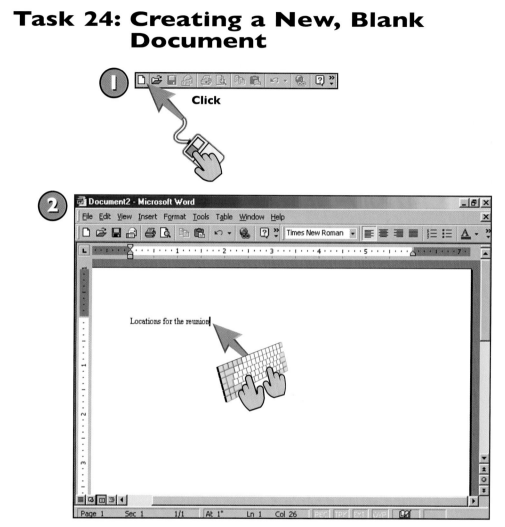

Click

Creating a New Document

When you want to create a brand-new document, you begin by opening a new document file. Word offers different ways to do this. The simplest method creates a blank file that uses default settings for margins, text font and size, and other features. Word assigns a temporary name to each new document you create: *Document1*, *Document2*, and so on. (When you start Word, it automatically opens a new, blank *Document1* document.) You must save the document to give it a unique name.

① Click the **New** button on the Standard toolbar.

② Start entering content in the new document.

WARNING
You also can choose **File, New** to create a new document. However, doing so requires extra steps. See Task 26 for illustrations regarding this method.

Task 25: Opening a Document You Created Earlier

Opening an Existing Document

After you create, save, and close a file, you don't have access to it. If you want to make changes to the file or print it, you need to open it in Word. You tell Word which file to open and where it's stored, and then Word redisplays it. After you make any changes, don't forget to click the **Save** button to save those changes.

✓ A File's Path

The disk, folder, and filename combined form the *path* to the file. For example, if you've saved a file named **Study Guide** in the School folder on your hard disk drive (C:), that file's path is `C:\School\Study Guide`. Note that you use backslash characters to separate the parts of the path.

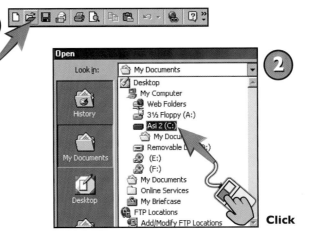

Click

Click

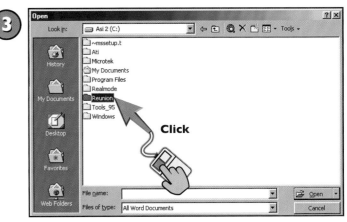

Click

(1) Click the **Open** button on the Standard toolbar.

(2) If you previously saved the file to a disk or folder other than the one that appears, click it in the **Look In** list.

(3) If the disk or folder you selected contains other folders, double-click the one that holds the file to open in the list.

Next Step

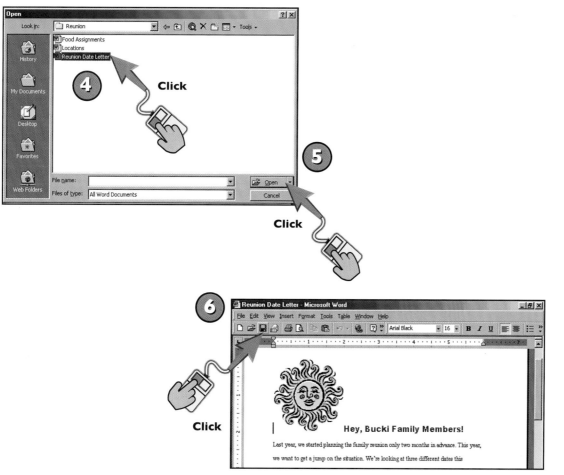

Using Caution with Floppies

If you're opening a file that's on a floppy disk (or other removable disk), be sure you insert the disk in the drive before you start the process for opening a file. Otherwise, you see a message that Word can't find the disk. It's also preferable to save a copy of the file to your hard disk and work on that copy. The hard disk provides Word with more "working space" for the file, possibly preventing file corruption. Plus, it's never a good policy to store files only on floppy disk; safely within your system, your hard disk tends to be a safer storage area.

④ Click the icon beside the file to open to select the file.

⑤ Click the **Open** button.

⑥ To resave the file after you've worked with it, click the **Save** button on the Standard toolbar.

Creating a Document from a Template

You can use **Word 2000** *templates* to create particular types of documents. Templates generally include attractive formatting. Some include starter text or prompt you to enter text in particular locations. Others also include graphical elements. Word organizes templates in categories.

🛇 WARNING

You can't use the New button on the Standard toolbar to create a document file based on a template. That button creates a blank document file.

✅ Learn About Wizards

If the template you think you want includes "Wizard" in its name, it's actually an automated template called a Wizard. Learn more about document Wizards in Task 27.

Task 26: Creating a Document from a Template

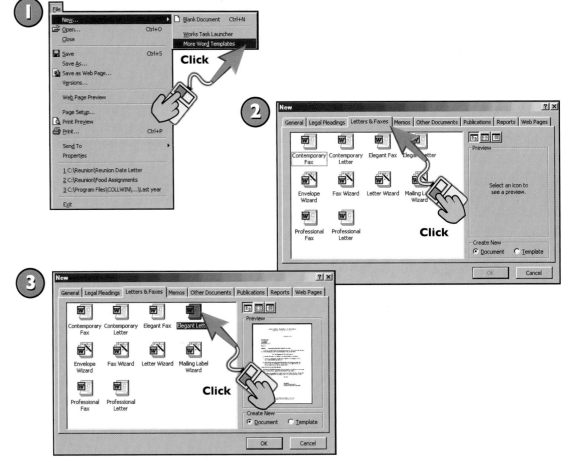

① Choose **File**, **New, More Word Templates**.

② Click the tab for the template category you want in order to see the templates in that category.

③ Click the icon for a template to see a preview of it at the left.

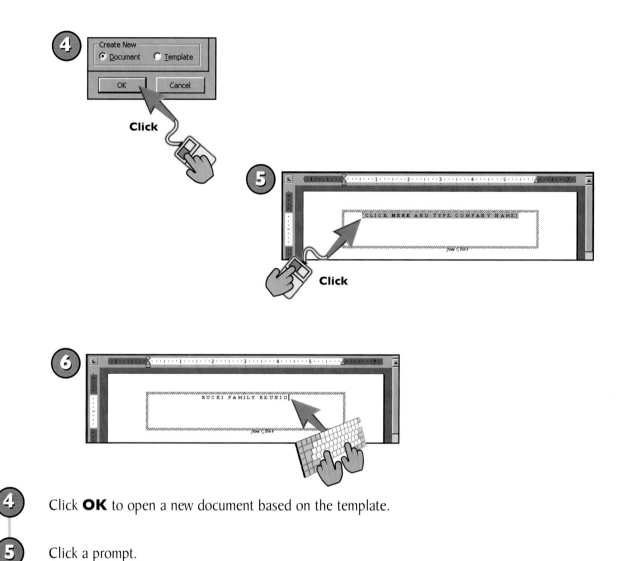

Finding Family Projects

As you'll learn in the first four tasks in Part 2, you can start Word and the other Works Suite applications from the Works Suite (Microsoft Works) Task Launcher. When you start Word from the Works Suite Task Launcher, you can use a Works task (project) to create fun documents such as certificates and flyers. You can choose **File, New, Works Task Launcher** in Word to start the Task Launcher and find the Word tasks.

4 Click **OK** to open a new document based on the template.

5 Click a prompt.

6 Type to fill in the prompt, and then click outside of it to finish using it.

Creating a Document Using a Wizard

In Word, *wizards* offer you the same benefits as templates, helping you to create a preformatted document and add your information in the correct places. A wizard includes the added benefit of automation. It walks you through the document creation process, not only letting you make choices about how the document looks but also enabling you to enter some information via dialog boxes rather than skimming through the document to find prompts (areas in a document that cue you to enter information) to fill in.

Task 27: Creating a Document Using a Wizard

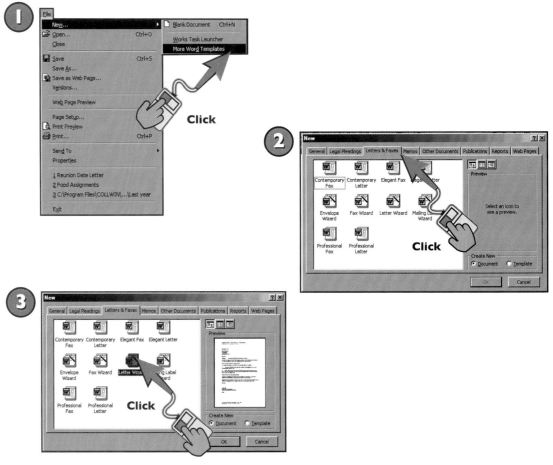

Choose **File**, **New**, **More Word Templates**.

Click the tab for the category you want in order to see the templates and wizards in that category.

Click the icon for the wizard you want in order to see a preview of it at the left.

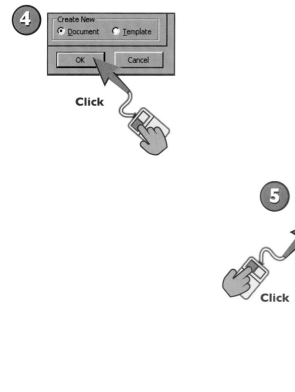

Click

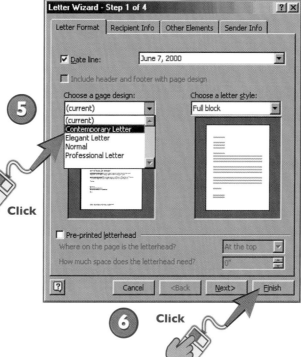

Click

Click

Continuing the Wizard

If the **Office Assistant** pops up after you select a wizard, click one of the choices in its bubble to continue the wizard. Next, right-click on the **Office Assistant** and click **Hide** to close it.

④ Click **OK** to start the Wizard.

⑤ Make the choices you want about how the document looks and enter document information in the various tabs of the wizard dialog box.

⑥ Click **Finish** to close the wizard and create the new document with the options you specified.

✔️ **Clicking Next to Move On**
Some wizards present multiple dialog boxes. After you make your choices in each dialog box, click the **Next** button to continue.

End Task

Changing Between Print Layout and Normal Views

The view controls how the document and Word appear onscreen. If you want to focus on plain paragraphs of text, use the Normal view. If you want to see how your document will look when printed, choose the Print Layout view. The Print Layout view displays a number of things you won't see in the Normal view, such as a vertical ruler, how margins appear, and other document features you might at some point experiment with, such as headers and footers or columns.

✅ **Click to View**
The four buttons at the left end of the horizontal toolbar also enable you to change views.

Task 28: Changing Between Print Layout and Normal Views

Start Here

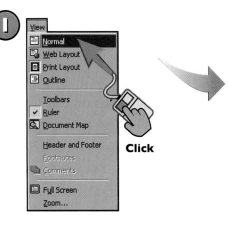

Click

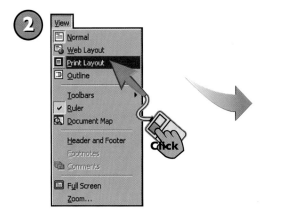

Click

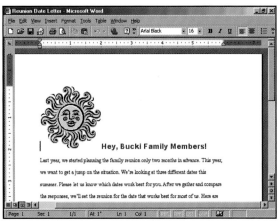

1 From the Print Layout view, choose **View**, **Normal** to display Normal view.

2 From the Normal view, choose **View**, **Print Layout** to display Print Layout view.

Task 29: Printing a Document

Start Here

Click

Click

Printing a Document

When you want a paper copy of your document, you need to print it. You can save time by printing multiple copies at once. Be sure your printer is turned on and has paper before you print. If you have trouble printing, check to be sure the printer cable is plugged in all the way.

(!) WARNING
If you just click the **Print** button on the Standard toolbar, Word prints only one copy of the document, using the default print settings.

(✓) Finding More Print Option Information
The Print dialog box offers other choices not covered here, such as the Collate check box or the Pages text box. To find out about any of the other options in the Print dialog box, click the **question mark (?)** button in the upper-right corner of the dialog box, and then click the option.

Choose **File**, **Print** (**Ctrl+P**).

Type a new value for the **Number of Copies** text box. (It's selected by default.)

Click **OK** to finish the print job.

End Task

Tackling Other Tasks with Works Suite 2000

The Microsoft Works Suite includes the software tools that form Microsoft Works (spreadsheet, database, and calendar) in addition to all the other applications in the suite. These tools enable you to use your computer to gather and track a number of different types of information: numbers and calculations, lists of information, or your upcoming appointments and events. The tasks in this part give you a gentle introduction to the Works Suite and Works tools, including the Works Suite Task Launcher.

Tasks

Opening and Closing Works

To access an individual Works tool or one of the other Works Suite programs, you need to start the Works Suite program itself. Starting Works Suite displays its Task Launcher, which you can use to create a new preformatted document by using a Task or to select a program or tool to create a blank document. When you've finished working with Works Suite, you can exit the Task Launcher.

✓ **Use the Start Menu**
To use the Start menu to launch Works Suite, click **Start**, point to **Programs**, and then click **Microsoft Works**.

🛇 **WARNING**
Closing the Task Launcher doesn't close an open Works tool or any other Works Suite application. You need to save files and close applications separately.

Task 1: Starting and Exiting Works (Works Suite)

Click

②

Click

 Double-click the **Microsoft Works** shortcut on the Windows Desktop.

② Choose **File**, **Exit Works** from the Task Launcher to close Works (Works Suite).

Task 2: Redisplaying the Task Launcher

Start
Here

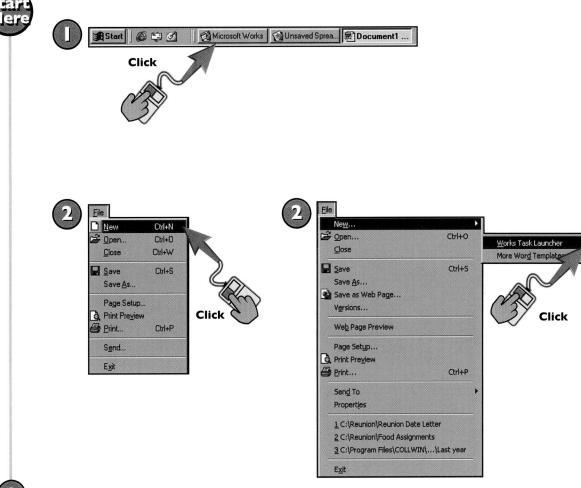

Opening the Task Launcher

After you open or create a file in Works, Task Launcher minimizes to a taskbar icon. The screen displays the Works tool (spreadsheet or database) or other Works Suite application that you've opened. To start a file using the another tool or application, you can redisplay the Task Launcher, using one of the two methods described in this task.

① Click the **Microsoft Works** button on the Windows taskbar.

② Choose **File**, **New** (**Ctrl+N**) from within the Works spreadsheet or database tool, or **File**, **New**, **Works Task Launcher** from Word.

✓ Displaying Another File

If you have several open files in more than one Works tool or Works Suite application, you can switch between the files and applications. To do so, click the appropriate button on the Windows taskbar.

End
Task

Task 3: Working with the Help Window

Using Works Help

When you're working in the Works spreadsheet, database, or calendar tools, you might see that the right side of the screen includes a special Works Help window. This window lists a menu of Help topics that apply to the Works tool you're using. You can use the Help window to display steps for performing a Works operation. Or, you can hide the Help window if you want to be able to see and work with more of the open file onscreen.

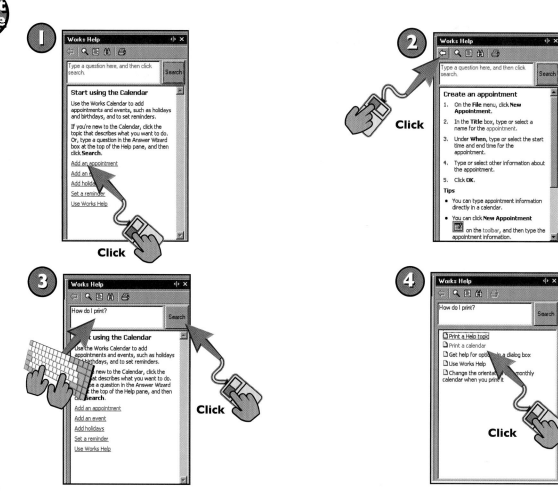

Start Here

Click

Click

Click

Click

✓ **Unhiding Help**
If you don't see the Help window, choose **Help, Works Help** or press **F1** to redisplay Help.

1 Click the topic you want help with.

2 After you review the help, click the **Back** button to return to the initial Works Help contents.

3 If you have a question, type it in the search text box, and click **Search**.

4 Click the topic you would like to review.

Next Step

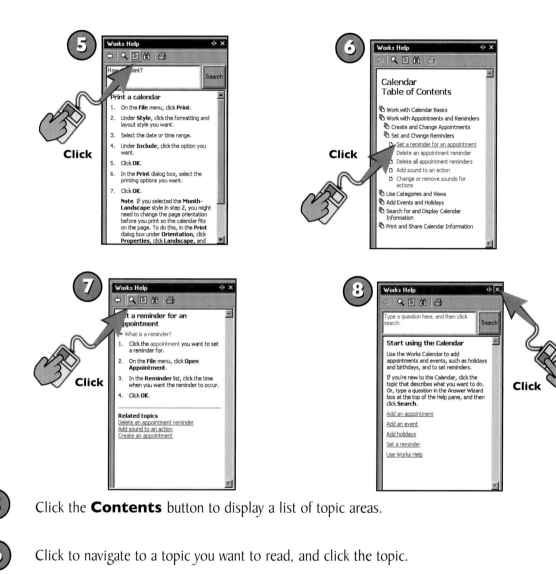

Finding Help About a Topic

Click the **Index** button to display a Help window that enables you to search for a term. To find help about a particular topic, type it in the text box at the top and then double-click the matching topic in the **Or Double-Click a Word** list below the text box. Click a topic in the list that appears at the bottom of the window.

---

5 Click the **Contents** button to display a list of topic areas.

6 Click to navigate to a topic you want to read, and click the topic.

7 Click the **Answer Wizard** button to return to the initial Works Help contents.

8 Click the **Close Help (X)** button in the upper-right corner to completely close Help.

✔ **Help Window Sizing**
Click the **Resize Help** button in the upper-right corner of the Works Help window to make the window more narrow or wide. You also can drag the divider bar at the left to adjust the window's size.

End Task

Task 4: Creating a New Document with a Task

Getting Help
Starting a Document

Through Works Suite, you can launch Microsoft Word to create text-based documents such as letters, résumés, flyers, and certificates. If you want a leg up starting a new document file, you can use a *task*, which designs the document and prompts you where to enter your information. (Works Suite does still have the Works word processor, but it uses Word to create documents. You can start the Works word processor by running the `C:\Program Files\ Microsoft Works\WksWP.exe` file.)

✓ Finding a Task

Click **Tasks** at the top of the Task Launcher to see tasks listed by category. Click the category you want in the list at the left, and then click one of the choices that appear to the right.

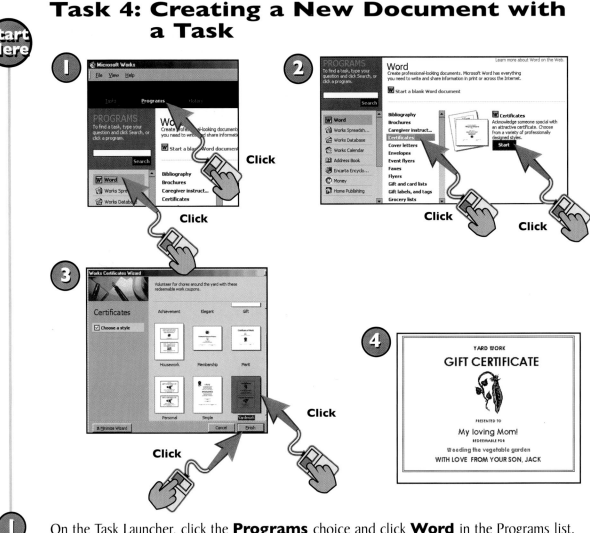

Start Here

Click

Click

Click

Click

Click

Click

YARD WORK
GIFT CERTIFICATE

PRESENTED TO
My loving Mom!
REDEEMABLE FOR
Weeding the vegetable garden
WITH LOVE FROM YOUR SON, JACK

1. On the Task Launcher, click the **Programs** choice and click **Word** in the Programs list.

2. Click the desired task in the list at the right, and then click **Start**.

3. Click a style for the document, and then click **Finish**.

4. Edit the new document (see Part I).

End Task

Task 5: Starting a Blank Word Document from Works Suite

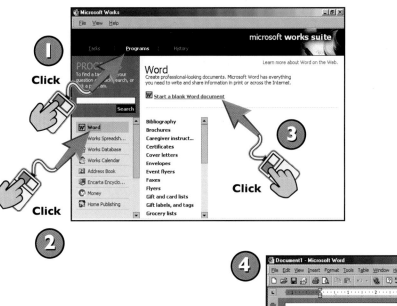

Start Here

Click

Click

Click

Opening an Application from the Task Launcher

The Works Suite Task Launcher can serve as a launching point for all the Works Suite applications, as well as the Works spreadsheet, database, and calendar tools. So, as you'll learn in this task, you can start Word (or any other suite application) from the Task Launcher to create a blank document or file.

1 On the Task Launcher, click the **Programs** choice.

2 Click **Word** in the Programs list.

3 Click **Start a Blank Word Document**.

4 Create the new document (see Part I).

✓ **Do the Suite**
To see all the programs in Works Suite, scroll down the Programs list and choose the one you'd like to start.

Using a Task to Create a Spreadsheet

You use the Works spreadsheet tool primarily to work with numerical values and labels for them. After you enter your values, you can enter a formula to calculate the data. The spreadsheet tool stores your values in a spread-sheet file. You can use a task to create a spreadsheet that already contains labels, formulas, and formatting. After you create a spread-sheet from a task, all you need to do is enter your values.

✅ Identifying Task Applications

When you click the **Tasks** choice in the Task Launcher, click a task category in the list at the left, and then click on a task, the description that appears at the far right includes the icon for the Works Suite application or Works tool.

Task 6: Creating a New Spreadsheet with a Task

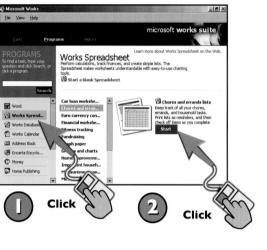

Click **Click**

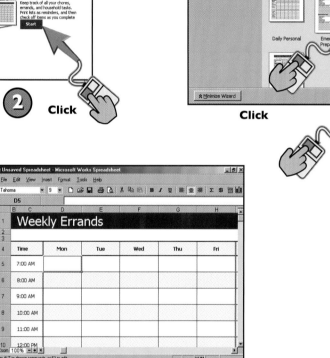

Click **Click**

(1) On the Task Launcher, click the **Programs** choice and click **Works Spreadsheet** in the Programs list.

(2) Click the desired task in the list at the right, and click **Start**.

(3) Click a style for the spreadsheet, and click **Finish**.

(4) Edit the new spreadsheet (see Tasks 8 through 22).

End
Task

Task 7: Creating a Blank Spreadsheet in the Spreadsheet Tool

Start Here

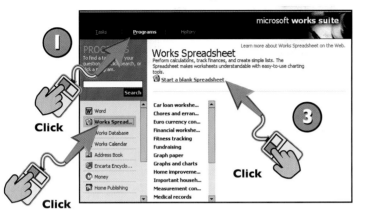

Opening a Blank Spreadsheet

If there's no task that creates the type of spreadsheet you need, you can create a blank spreadsheet to start from scratch.

① On the Task Launcher, click the Programs choice.

② Click Works Spreadsheet in the Programs list.

③ Click Start a Blank Spreadsheet.

④ Create the new spreadsheet (see Tasks 8 through 22).

✓ **Quick 'n' New**
If you've already started the spreadsheet tool, click the **New** button on its toolbar to create a blank spreadsheet without returning to the Task Launcher.

✓ **Back to the Launch Pad**
Choose File, **New** to return from the spreadsheet tool to the Task Launcher.

End Task

Task 8: Entering Text in a Spreadsheet

Creating Spreadsheet Text

Each spreadsheet consists of a grid of rows and columns that intersect to form *cells*. You type each spreadsheet entry into a separate cell. A black cell selector highlights the current cell, where your entry will appear. The spreadsheet tool treats text entries (also called *labels* for your data) differently from numerical and date entries. For starters, text lines up at the left side of the cell. The spreadsheet automatically inserts a left double prime (") to the left of a label entry to identify the entry as text. And the spreadsheet won't calculate cells containing text because it can only calculate values.

✔ **Finishing Any Cell Entry**
Whether entering text or a number (value), you can finish the entry by clicking the **Check Mark** button on the Entry bar, by pressing **Tab**, or by pressing **Enter**.

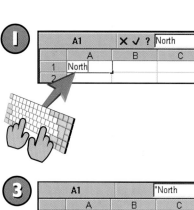

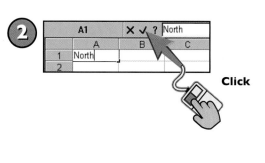

Click

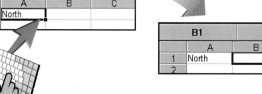

1 Type a label entry in the current cell.

2 Click the **Check Mark** button on the Entry bar to finish the entry.

3 Press **Tab** or the **Right Arrow** to move one cell right or the **Down Arrow** to move one cell down.

4 Type another entry and press **Tab** to move to the next cell or **Enter** to finish it.

Task 9: Entering Numbers and Dates in a Spreadsheet

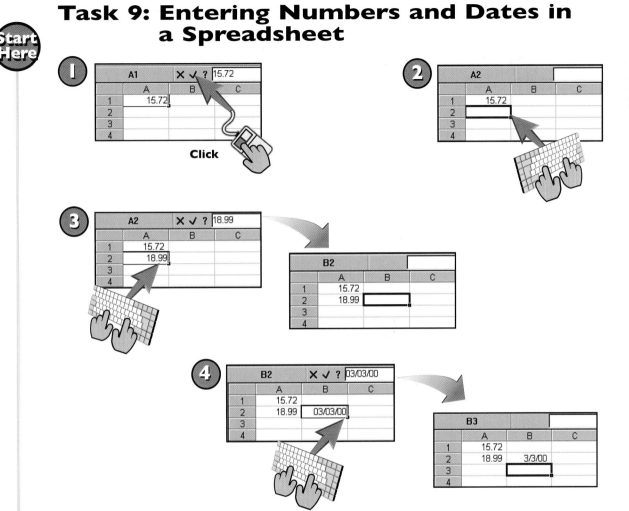

Click

Typing Numbers and Dates in a Spreadsheet

Numbers form the core of every spreadsheet. When you enter a number or date in a cell, it lines up at the right side of the cell. When you enter a number, type a period to indicate the decimal point, as well as any digits to the right of the decimal point. You can apply special formats to cells holding numbers, controlling such aspects as how many decimal points display and whether a dollar sign is included. See Task 20 to learn about number formatting.

✓ **Dealing with Wide Cell Entries**

If a number or date you enter into a cell displays as a series of pound signs (###), the entry is too wide. (Text entries just spill over the adjacent right cell.) You can change the column width to display the full number (see Task 19).

1. Type a number entry in the current cell and click the **Check Mark** button on the entry bar to finish the entry.

2. Press **Tab** or **Right Arrow** to move one cell right or the **Down Arrow** to move one cell down.

3. Type another entry and press **Tab** to finish it and move one cell to the right.

4. Type a date and press **Enter** to finish it.

Navigating to a Cell

The *cell reference* (or *cell address*) identifies each cell in the spreadsheet. The cell's column letter and row number combine to form its reference. That is, the cell in row 4 of column **B** is cell **B4**. The left side of the entry bar (below the toolbar in the spreadsheet) displays the reference for the current (selected) cell. Entries or changes you make appear in the current cell. This task shows you how to move around the spreadsheet to select a cell with either the mouse or keyboard in preparation for your entries and edits.

✓ **Moving with the Keyboard**

Press **Ctrl+Home** to go to cell **A1**. Press **Ctrl+End** to display the last cell in the spreadsheet containing data. Pressing **Home** or **End** goes to the first or last cell in the row that contains data, respectively.

Task 10: Moving Around in the Spreadsheet

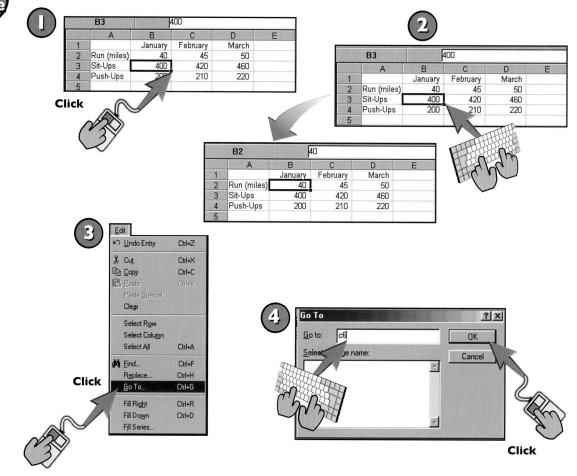

Start Here

Click

Click

Click

Click

1. Click any cell to select it.

2. Press an arrow key to move one column or row in the direction of the arrow.

3. Choose **Edit**, **Go To** (**Ctrl+G**).

4. Type the cell reference for the cell to select in the Go To text box and click **OK**.

End Task

Task 11: Selecting a Range, Row, or Column

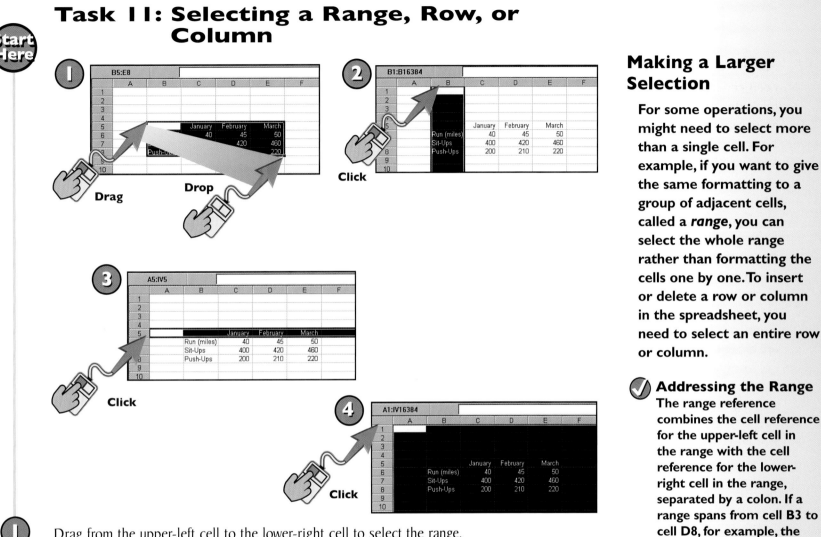

Drag

Drop

Click

Click

Click

Making a Larger Selection

For some operations, you might need to select more than a single cell. For example, if you want to give the same formatting to a group of adjacent cells, called a *range*, you can select the whole range rather than formatting the cells one by one. To insert or delete a row or column in the spreadsheet, you need to select an entire row or column.

✓ **Addressing the Range**
The range reference combines the cell reference for the upper-left cell in the range with the cell reference for the lower-right cell in the range, separated by a colon. If a range spans from cell **B3** to cell **D8**, for example, the range reference is **B3:D8**.

✓ **The Keyboard**
You also can press and hold the **Shift** key and press one or more arrow keys to select a range.

1. Drag from the upper-left cell to the lower-right cell to select the range.

2. Click a column letter to select the entire column.

3. Click a row letter to select the entire row.

4. Click the gray button above the row 1 row number to select the entire spreadsheet.

Task 12: Building a Basic Formula with Easy Calc

Using Easy Calc to Enter a Formula

A formula performs calculations on the values you've entered into spreadsheet cells or on other numbers you enter into the formula. Each formula begins with an equal sign and uses the mathematical operators + (addition), – (subtraction), * (multiplication), and / (division). For example, **=A3+52** adds 52 to whatever value you entered in cell **A3**. Or, **=B2*B3** multiplies the values in those cells. Formulas also can use *functions*, which serve as shorthand for more complicated formulas and enable you to perform a calculation on a range. For example, you can use the Sum function to total a range, as in **=SUM(B2:B4)**. Rather than learning all the ins and outs of formulas and functions, you can use Easy Calc to help you build a formula.

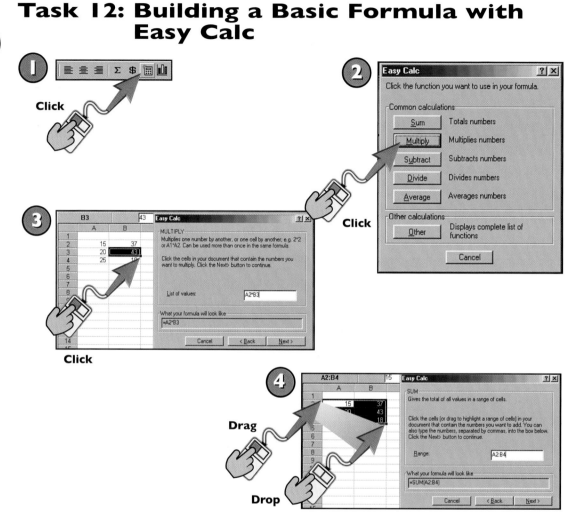

Click

Click

Click

Drag

Drop

1. Click the **Easy Calc** button on the toolbar.

2. Click the type of calculation you would like to perform.

3. If prompted to enter cell references in the formula, click each one to include in the spreadsheet.

4. If prompted to enter a range reference in the formula, drag over the range in the spreadsheet.

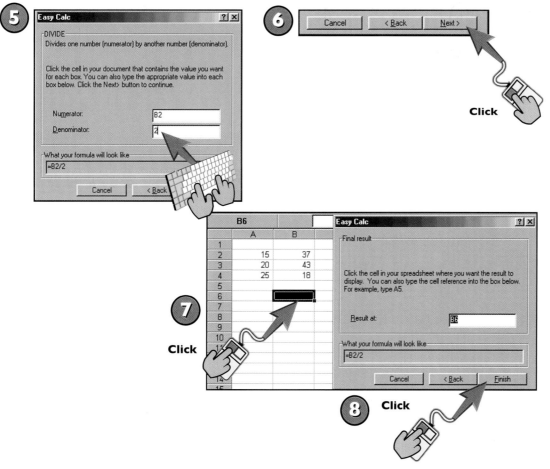

Controlling Calculation Order

By default, the spreadsheet tool multiplies and divides first and then adds and subtracts. It does not work from left to right as you would. To control the calculation order, use parentheses. Works calculates the information in the innermost pair of parentheses first, and then works outward. For example, Works would calculate the formula =5+7*(2+2) as 33, whereas the result would be 26 if you calculated from left to right.

⑤ If prompted to enter either or number or a cell reference, type the number or click to select a cell.

⑥ Click **Next**.

⑦ Click the cell that you want to hold the formula.

⑧ Click **Finish**.

✓ **Displaying a Formula**
The cell that holds the formula displays the calculated formula result, not the formula itself. When you select a cell containing a formula, the formula appears in the entry bar.

Task 13: Using a Function for a Calculation

Calculating with a Function

Functions are predefined formulas that perform a more complex calculation. A function performs its calculations on the arguments you specify. Each argument might be a value you enter or a cell or range reference. The Works spreadsheet offers dozens of functions. You do not need to remember each function and the arguments it requires. Instead, you can insert the function, and Works prompts you for the proper arguments.

✓ **Summing Up Cells**
Click the **AutoSum** button to enter a formula that sums the values above or to the left of the current cell.

✓ **Canceling an Entry**
Press **Esc** at any time to cancel a cell entry or function or formula you're entering.

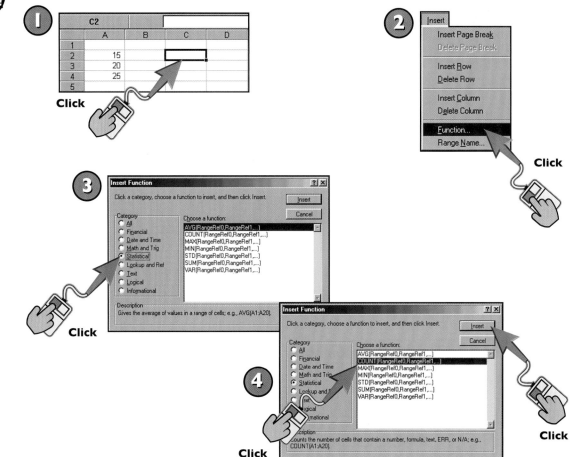

Click

Click

Click

Click

Click

1. Click to select the cell where you want to insert the formula with a function.

2. Choose **Insert**, **Function**.

3. Click the **Category** that contains the function to use.

4. Click the function to use in the **Choose a Function** list and click **Insert**.

Next Step

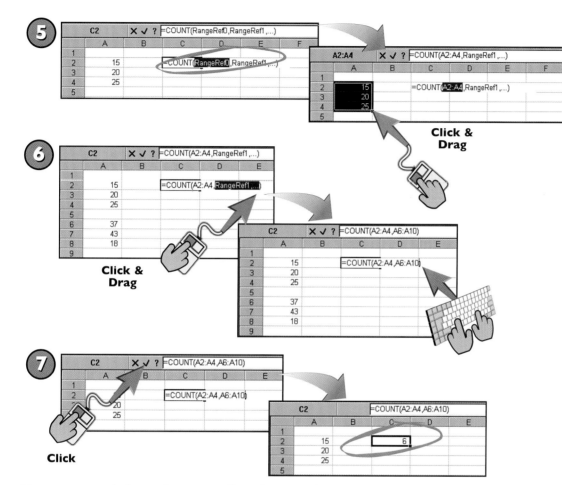

Click & Drag

Click & Drag

Click

Getting Arguments Right

Be sure to enter arguments just as prompted by Works. For example, if an argument calls for a percentage but you specify a cell that doesn't display the intended percentage, the calculation results will be wrong. You also might need to divide a percentage rate by 12 (as in 7.5%/12) to yield a monthly rate. If you specify an argument entry that won't work at all, Works displays an error message.

✓ Entering Needed Arguments

Works inserts the arguments within parentheses and uses a comma to separate arguments. If there's an ellipsis (...) after the last argument, you can enter as many arguments as you want, separating each with a comma. If there's no ellipsis, enter only those arguments specified by the inserted function formula.

5 Type an entry, click to select one cell or drag to select a range to fill in the first, highlighted (by default) argument.

6 Drag over the next argument and type the next value, cell, or range reference to fill it in. Repeat this process for subsequent arguments.

7 Click the check on the entry bar to finish entering the formula.

End Task

Task 14: Editing a Cell

Changing Cell Contents

As information changes, you may find that you need to adjust the entries on your spreadsheet. Your electronic spreadsheet is much easier to update than a paper ledger. You can either completely retype a cell entry, or you can edit a longer entry, such as a formula, to correct it.

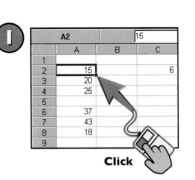

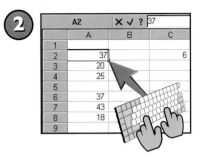

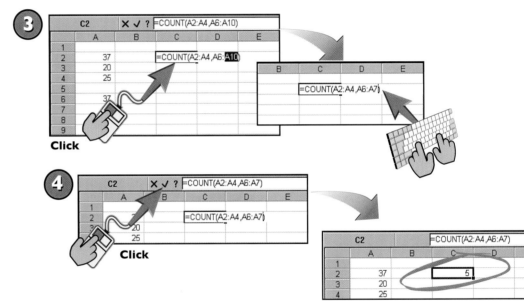

✅ **Editing in the Entry Bar**

You can click the cell to edit and then click in the entry bar to make your changes there.

① Click the cell to edit.

② Type the new entry and click the check mark on the Entry bar or press **Enter**.

③ Double-click a cell that holds a longer entry, and then drag over the portion of the entry to edit and type your changes.

④ Click the check mark on the entry bar or press **Enter** to finish.

Task 15: Undoing a Change

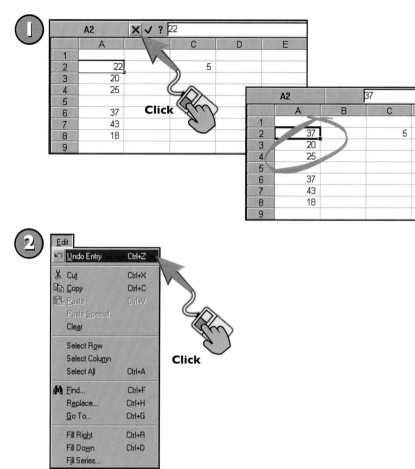

Click

Edit
↺	Undo Entry	Ctrl+Z
✂	Cut	Ctrl+X
📋	Copy	Ctrl+C
📋	Paste	Ctrl+V
	Paste Special...	
	Clear	
	Select Row	
	Select Column	
	Select All	Ctrl+A
🔍	Find...	Ctrl+F
	Replace...	Ctrl+H
	Go To...	Ctrl+G
	Fill Right	Ctrl+R
	Fill Down	Ctrl+D
	Fill Series...	

Click

1 Press **Esc** or click the **X** on the entry bar to cancel an in-progress edit.

2 To undo the previous change, choose **Edit**, **Undo (Action)**. The command changes based on the last change you made.

Using Undo

Editing and formatting your spreadsheet can be an imperfect process. You might change an entry or formula and find you've introduced an inaccuracy. Or, you might be experimenting with the look of your spreadsheet and decide you don't like a formatting change you just made. You can cancel or undo an entry or change, if needed.

⚠ WARNING
Unlike Word, which enables you to undo multiple previous changes, Works tools enable you to undo only the change you just made. So, you must use the Undo command immediately in the spreadsheet.

✓ Database Undo
The Works database tool also offers the Undo command. **Ctrl+Z** is the shortcut combination for the Undo command.

Task 16: Adding Boldface, Italic, or Underlining to a Selection

Adding Attributes to Cells

To emphasize certain cells in the spreadsheet, you can change their formatting. You can start out by applying **boldface**, *italic*, or underlining to the text labels you enter in a spreadsheet to call attention to those labels.

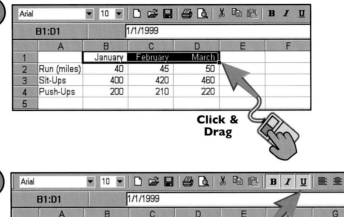

Start Here

Click & Drag

Click

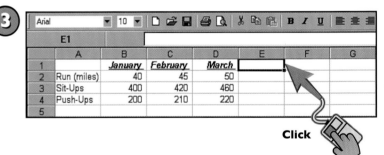

Click

✓ **Removing Attributes**
To remove boldface, italic, or underlining you've previously applied to a cell, select the cell and click the **Bold, Italic,** or **Underline** button to remove the desired formatting.

✓ **Keyboard Shortcuts for Formatting**
Press **Ctrl+B** to apply or remove boldface, **Ctrl+I** to apply or remove italic, and **Ctrl+U** to apply or remove underlining.

1 Select the cell or range to format.

2 Click the **Bold** button, the **Italic** button, and the **Underline** button.

3 Click outside the selection to see your changes.

End Task

Task 17: Choosing a New Font and Size for a Selection

Start Here

1

| Arial | ▼ | 10 | ▼ | | | | | | | | |

A2:A4		"Run (miles)		

	A	B	C	D	E
1		January	February	March	
2	Run (miles)	40	45	50	
3	Sit-Ups	400	420	460	
4	Push-Ups	200	210	220	
5					

Click & Drag

2

| Chiller | ▼ |

- 𝕋 Calisto MT
- 𝕋 CASTELLAR
- 𝕋 Century Gothic
- 𝕋 Chiller
- 𝕋 Comic Sans MS
- 𝕋 **Cooper Black**

Click

3

| 10 | ▼ |

6
8
10
12
14
16
18
20
24
30
32
36
40
48

Click

4

| Arial | ▼ | 10 | ▼ | | | | | | | | |

A5				

	A	B	C	D	E
1		January	February	March	
2	Run (miles)	40	45	50	
3	Sit-Ups	400	420	460	
4	Push-Ups	200	210	220	
5					
6					

Click

1 Select the cell or range to format.

2 Open the **Font Name** drop-down list and click a new font to apply it.

3 Open the **Font Size** drop-down list and click a new size to apply it.

4 Click outside the selection to see your changes.

Changing the Font and Size for Cell Contents

You can change the font (letter style) used by a cell's contents or increase the font size. When you increase the font size, the spreadsheet tool automatically increases or decreases the row height as needed. However, it does not increase the column width, which means your text entries might get cut off at the right (if the next cell right contains an entry), or number or formula entries might display as a string of pound signs (###). To redisplay the full entry, you can increase the column width, as described in Task 19.

✓ AutoFormatting a Spreadsheet

The Works spreadsheet offers *AutoFormats*—predefined formatting combinations you can apply to a selection. To apply an AutoFormat to a selection, choose **Format, AutoFormat**.

End Task

Task 18: Changing Cell Alignment

Aligning Cell Contents

In word processors, you can change how paragraphs line up relative to the left and right margins (horizontal alignment). In the spreadsheet tool, you control how cell entries line up relative to the borders of the cell, including the top and bottom borders (called the *vertical alignment*). Also, the spreadsheet's Alignment tab in the Format Cells dialog box offers some special formatting choices, described in this task. The General alignment changes the cell's horizontal alignment depending on the type of entry (lining up text to the left and numbers to the right).

✓ **Using the Format Cells Dialog Box**
After you display the Format Cells dialog box, you can click any of its tabs and change other formatting settings before clicking **OK** to close the dialog box and apply your choices.

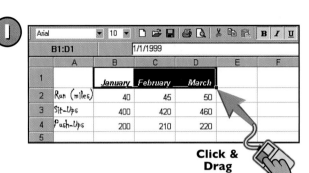

Click & Drag

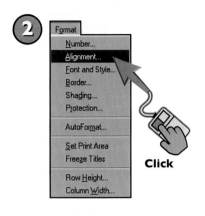

Click

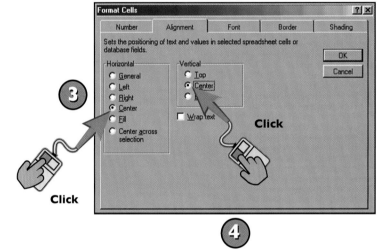

Click

Click

Click

1 Select the cell or range to format.

2 Choose **Format**, **Alignment**.

3 Click a choice in the **Horizontal** area of the Alignment tab to determine the horizontal alignment.

4 Click a choice in the **Vertical** area of the Alignment tab to determine the vertical alignment.

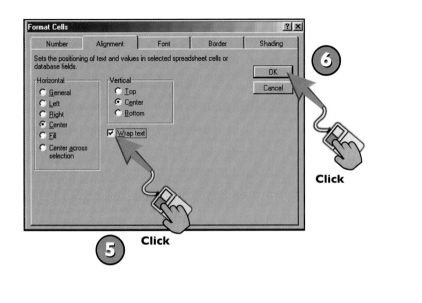

Click

Click

Click

Using Other Alignments

The **Fill** choice repeats the cell entry to fill the cell's width. The **Center Across Selection** choice centers the entry in the first cell of a range across the entire range. That is, if you want to center a lengthy cell entry across three cells, select a range that includes the entry plus two cells to the right before applying this choice. The **Wrap Text** choice divides a lengthy cell entry into several lines within the cell and increases the row height so that all of the entry can display in the cell.

5 Click to check the **Wrap Text** check box if you need to wrap long entries in the selection.

6 Click the **OK** button to close the dialog box and apply your alignment settings.

7 Click outside the selection to see your changes.

✓ Using Alignment Buttons
You can quickly change the selection's horizontal alignment by clicking the **Left Align**, **Center Align**, or **Right Align** button on the spreadsheet tool's toolbar.

End Task

Adjusting Columns and Rows

An entry or formatting change can cause a cell to be cut off at the right or displayed as pound signs because it can't fit in the cell. This Task presents the fix for that problem and other situations where you might want to change the width of one or more columns and the height of one or more rows.

✅ **Fine-Tuning Sizing**
The Row Height and Column Width dialog boxes work identically. In addition to specifying a precise column width (in characters) or row height (in points), you can click the **Standard** button to return the row height or column width to the default. Click **Best Fit** to size the selected columns (or rows) to fit the widest (or tallest) entry in the column (or row).

Task 19: Changing Column Width or Row Height

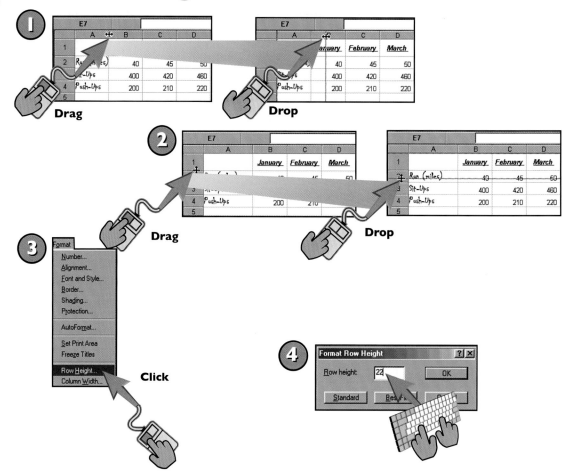

Point to the border to the right of the column letter for the column to resize or below the row number for the row to resize.

Drag the column border horizontally or the row border vertically and release the mouse to finish resizing.

Alternatively, click a cell in the column or row to resize and choose **Format**, **Column Width** or **Format**, **Row Height**.

Enter the new column width or row height and click **OK**.

Task 20: Changing the Number Format

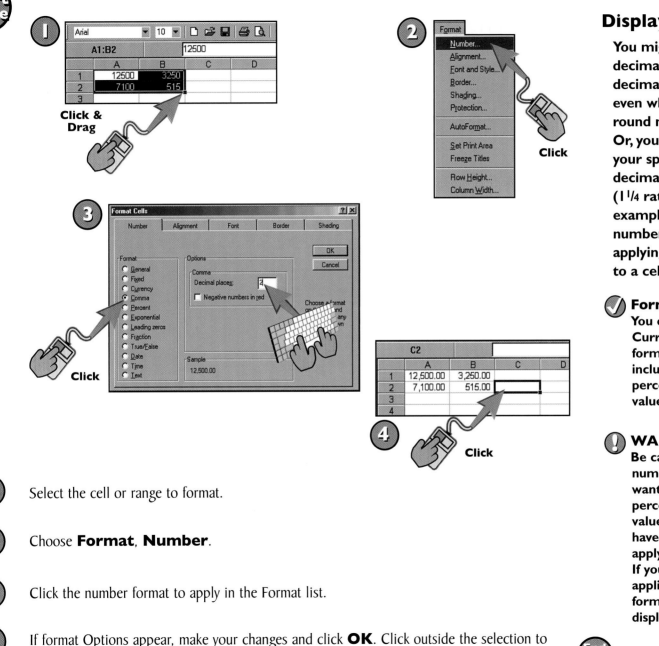

Displaying Numbers

You might want to display a decimal point and two decimal places with a value, even when you enter a round number (as in **25.00**). Or, you might want to have your spreadsheet display decimal values as fractions (1¼ rather than 1.25, for example). Specify special number formatting by applying a *number format* to a cell.

✓ Formatting On-the-Fly

You can apply the Currency and Percent formats as you type by including a dollar sign or a percent sign with the value, as in **$25** or **25%**.

① WARNING

Be careful when you enter numbers that you later want to format as percentages. If you want a value to read "75%," you have to enter .75 before applying a Percent format. If you entered **75** and applied the Percent format, the cell would display "7500%."

---

① Select the cell or range to format.

② Choose **Format**, **Number**.

③ Click the number format to apply in the Format list.

④ If format Options appear, make your changes and click **OK**. Click outside the selection to see your changes.

Shading and Outlining a Range

If a selection contains particularly significant or unique entries, you can call maximum attention to the selection by adding a border around it and some shading within it. You accomplish both of these tasks with the Format Cells dialog box.

Task 21: Adding a Border and Shading to a Range

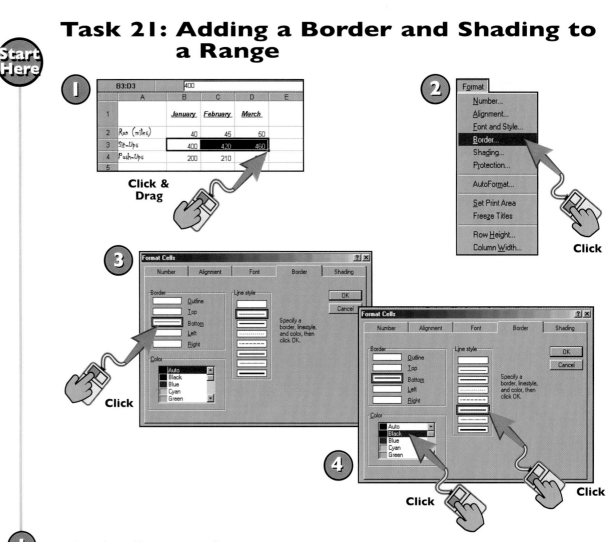

Start Here

Click & Drag

Click

Click

Click

Click

Shading a Range Only
If you want to apply shading but no border to a cell, you can save a little time by choosing **Format, Shading** to go directly to the Shading tab of the Format Cells dialog box.

1 Select the cell or range to format.

2 Choose **Format**, **Border**.

3 In the **Border** area, click the **Outline** choice or any combination of the other four choices.

4 Click a **Line Style** choice and click a **Color** choice.

Next Step

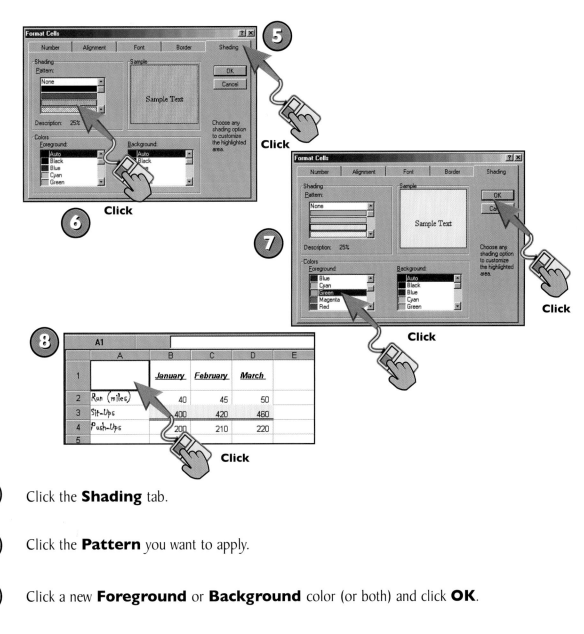

Removing Borders or Shading

Click the blank **Line Style** on the Border tab and then click one or more **Border** choices to remove a previously applied border. Or, click the **None Pattern** on the Shading tab to remove previously applied shading.

5 Click the **Shading** tab.

6 Click the **Pattern** you want to apply.

7 Click a new **Foreground** or **Background** color (or both) and click **OK**.

8 Click outside the selection to see your changes.

Charting Values

Although your spreadsheet entries have all the precision you want, they don't necessarily clarify how the entries relate. You can more clearly see trends or how the different values compare by charting your data. You can choose one of 12 different chart types.

✓ **Using Charting Commands**

A chart you create appears in place of the spreadsheet in the spreadsheet tool window. When the chart window is open onscreen, the Format and Tools menus change to offer commands for working with charts.

Task 22: Creating a Chart

Start Here

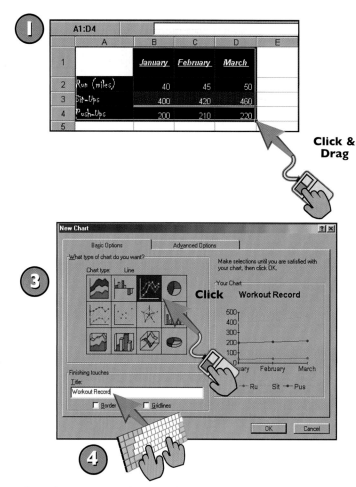

Click & Drag

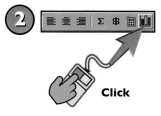

Click

Click   Workout Record

1. Select the range to chart, including row or column text that identifies your entries.

2. Click the **New Chart** button or choose **Tools**, **Create New Chart**. Click **To Create a Chart** if the First-Time Help window appears.

3. On the **Basic Options** tab, click the chart type you want. A preview appears at the right.

4. Enter a name to display on the chart in the **Title** text box.

Next Step

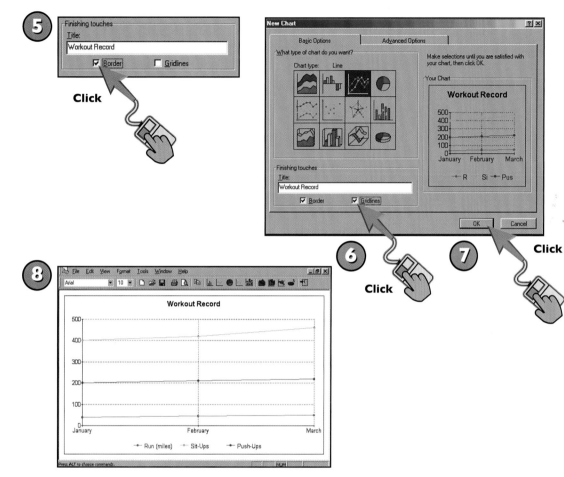

Viewing a Chart

After you add one or more charts to the spreadsheet and save the spreadsheet, you can redisplay the spreadsheet from the chart. To do so, open the **Window** menu and click the spreadsheet name. To redisplay the chart when you later open the spreadsheet file, choose **View, Chart** and double-click the chart to redisplay in the list. Choosing **File, Close** closes both the spreadsheet and any open charts for that spreadsheet.

Click the **Border** check box to add a border around the chart.

Click the **Gridlines** check box to add gridlines to set off the charted data.

Click **OK**.

Close the Help window, and work with the chart as needed.

Using a Task to Make a Database

You use the Works database tool to keep and organize lists of information. A database stores information in records and fields. For example, if you create an address book database, all the information about each person is a *record*, and each individual piece of information within a record (such as the last name) is a *field*. You can use a task to create a database with already defined fields so that you can begin entering records.

✓ **Finding a Database Task**

The Task Launcher identifies database TaskWizards with the database tool icon. Database tasks organize lists of information.

Task 23: Creating a New Database with a Task

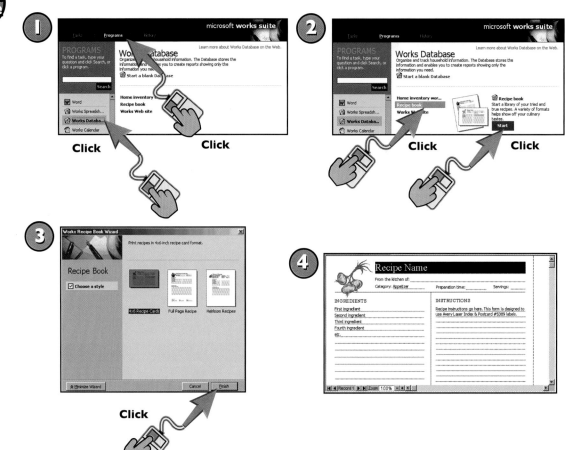

Start Here

Click   Click

Click   Click

Click

Click

① In the Task Launcher, click the **Programs** choice and click **Works Database** in the Programs list.

② Click the desired task in the list at the right, and then click **Start**.

③ Click a style for the database, and then click **Finish**.

④ Edit the new database (see Tasks 26 through 37).

End Task

Task 24: Filling In Records in Form View

Start Here

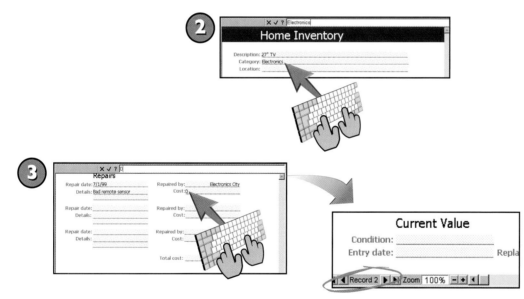

Using Form View to Enter Records

After you use a task to create a database, the data form appears and displays all the fields in the database. The data form is empty because the database contains no data until you enter some. The data form displays the fields in a spacious form with one record (all the fields for one entry) in a single page. The data form makes it easy to enter and review data record by record because the screen isn't cluttered with other records.

✓ **Finding the Active Field**

The field that's ready to accept an entry (the selected field) appears in a darker gray than the other fields. To go back to a previous field, click that field, press the left arrow key, or **Shift+Tab**. You can then simply type a new entry for the field.

1 Type the information for the first field and press **Tab** to select the next field.

2 Continue typing entries and pressing **Tab** to move to the next field.

3 Press **Tab** after you fill in the last field to complete the current record and start a new one.

Starting a Database from Scratch

Most of the database tasks include a lot of fields—often more fields than you need. If there's no task that creates a database with all the fields you need or if you want to create a simpler database with fewer fields, you can create a blank database from scratch.

Task 25: Creating a Blank Database with the Database Tool

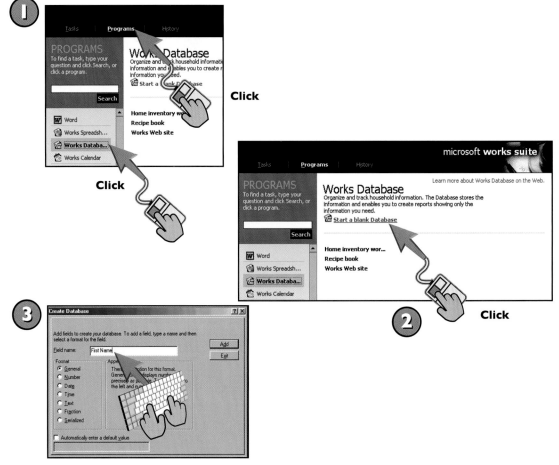

Click

Click

Click

Click

In the Task Launcher, click the **Programs choice and click **Works Database** in the Programs list.

Click **Start a Blank Database. Click **To Create a New Database** if the First-Time Help window appears.

Type the name for the first field in the **Field Name text box.

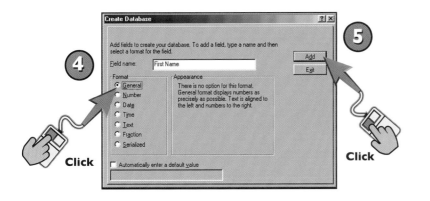

Determining the Right Format

For entries that contain only letters (such as names), use the **General** format. If an entry contains both numbers and special characters, such as a phone number, choose the **Text** format.

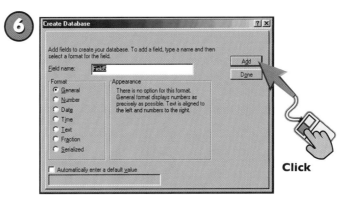

④ If needed, click the field type for the new field under **Format**.

⑤ Click **Add** to add the field.

⑥ Repeat steps 3 through 5 to add as many fields as you want; click **Done** to close the dialog box. Close the Help window.

Task 26: Filling In New Records in List View

Using the List View to Enter Records

After you create a blank database with the database tool, the data list appears and displays fields added in the database, as well as rows for multiple records. The data list is initially empty because the database contains no data until you enter some. Each row in a data list contains a single record. The compact list format enables you to display multiple records on a single page. In the list view, you can review multiple records without having to move back and forth between them.

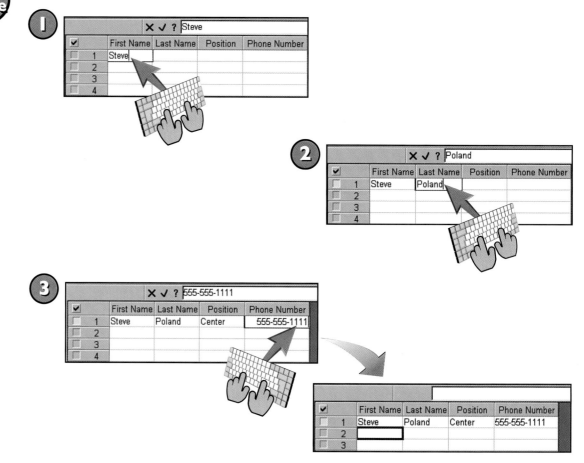

✓ Finding the Active Field
The field that's ready to accept an entry (the selected field) has a heavy cell selector border around it, just like in a Works spreadsheet.

Type the information for the first field and press **Tab** to select the next field.

Continue typing entries and pressing **Tab** to move to the next field.

Press **Tab** after you fill in the last field to complete the current record, moving the cell selector to the first field in the next record.

End Task

Task 27: Changing Between Form View and List View

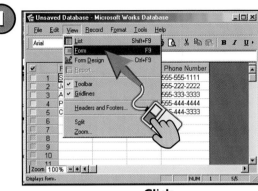

Click

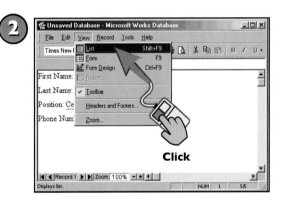

Click

1 Choose **View**, **Form** (**F9**) to change from the List view to the Form view.

2 Choose **View**, **List** (**Shift+F9**) to change from the Form view to the List view.

Choosing Form View or List View in the Database

Your preference alone dictates whether you need to enter and work with records in the data form (Form view) or data list (List view). You can easily switch to the view you need.

Printing a Database View

When you print your database file, Works prints the current view—the data form or the data list—so choose the view you want before you print. Task 39 explains how to print in a Works tool.

Task 28: Moving Between Records in Form View

Displaying a Different Record in Form View

List view makes it easy to move to the record you want. You can simply scroll to it and click it. The data form (Form view) doesn't make moving around so obvious. You have to use buttons to the left of the horizontal scrollbar to move between records in the Form view.

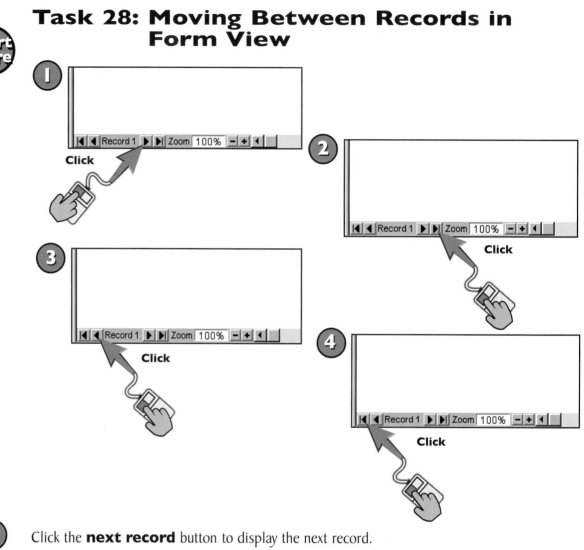

 Click the **next record** button to display the next record.

 Click the **last record** button to move to the end of the database, displaying a new, blank record.

 Click the **previous record** button to display the previous record.

 Click the **first record** button to display the very first record in the database.

Task 29: Using Go To to Jump to a Field

Click

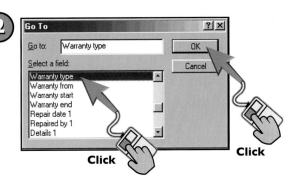

Click

Click

③

Warranty

Warranty type:
Warranty from:

Warranty start:
Warranty end:

Going to a Specific Field

You can think of the Form view as displaying a "page" of information at a time. If your database has too many fields to display onscreen and you want to jump between them in the Form view, you can use the Go To command to get there.

① With the record you want to navigate displayed, choose **Edit**, **Go To**.

② Click the field to go to in the **Select a Field** list and click **OK**.

③ Type a new field entry or view the entry in the selected field.

✅ **Go to a List Field**
You also can use the Go To command in List view. First, click in a field in the record you want to work with. Use Go To to select the field you want in that record.

✅ **Editing Field Contents**
To change the contents of the selected field, type a new entry and press **Tab**.

Task 30: Finding a Record

Using Find to Display a Record

If you have dozens or hundreds of records in your database, you don't have to sit and move through the records one by one to find a record you want. You can instead perform a find to display the record you need. You enter the information to match (from any field in the database) and then tell Works to display the next matching record or all matching records.

✓ Controlling the Find's Starting Point

You can perform a find in both the List view and the Form view. The Find operation starts from the currently displayed record, so if you want to be sure that Works examines all the records (if you find the next record instead of all of them), press **Ctrl+Home** to display the first record before performing the find.

Start Here

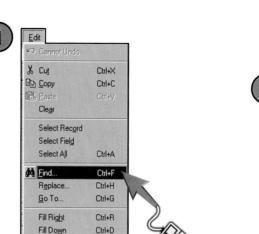

Click

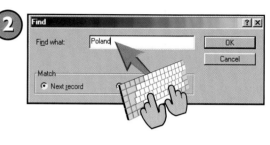

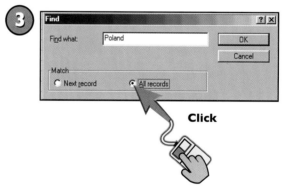

Click

① Choose **Edit**, **Find** (**Ctrl+F**).

② Type a field entry from the record(s) to find in the **Find What** text box.

③ If you want to find all the matching records rather than only the next match, click **All Records**, and then **OK**.

Next Step

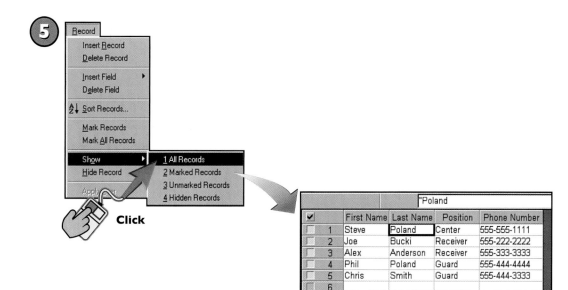

When you perform a find, Works marks the matching records and hides the unmarked records. You also can manually mark, unmark, hide, and redisplay records as described in Tasks 31–34.

4 You can review the matching record(s) in the view you want. (Use the navigation buttons to the left of the horizontal scrollbar in Form view.) Intervening records are hidden.

5 To redisplay all the database records, choose **Record**, **Show**, **All Records**.

Marking and Unmarking Records in Form View

Long databases can become unwieldy when you have to move through all the records to find the records that you would like to work with. When you perform a find, however, all the found records have to have a common entry in one of the fields. To display a list of records that don't necessarily match, you need to mark the records; then you can show only the marked or unmarked records in your database (see Task 33). This task explains how to mark (and unmark) records in Form view. The next task explains how to mark and unmark records in List view.

✓ **Checking a Record's Marking**
The only way to tell whether a record is marked in Form view is to open the Record menu and see whether Mark Record is checked.

Task 31: Marking and Unmarking Records in Form View

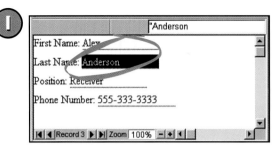

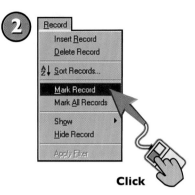

Click

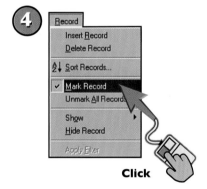

Click

1 Display a record to mark.

2 Choose **Record**, **Mark Record**. (Repeat steps 1 and 2 to mark additional records.)

3 Display a record to unmark.

4 Choose **Record**, **Mark Record** to clear the check beside that command. (Repeat steps 3 and 4 to unmark additional records.)

Task 32: Marking and Unmarking Records in List View

Start Here

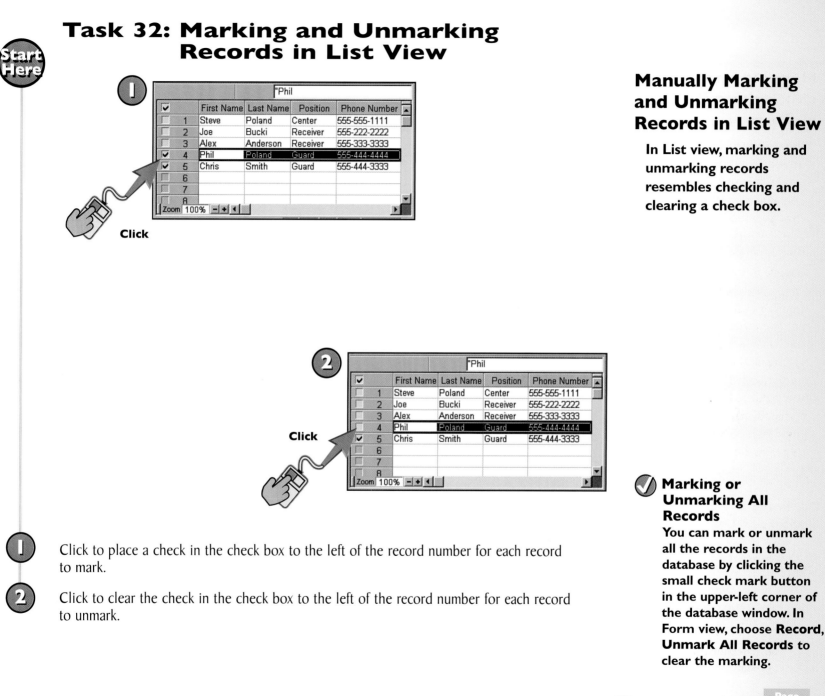

1

"Phil

		First Name	Last Name	Position	Phone Number
	1	Steve	Poland	Center	555-555-1111
	2	Joe	Bucki	Receiver	555-222-2222
	3	Alex	Anderson	Receiver	555-333-3333
✓	4	Phil	Poland	Guard	555-444-4444
✓	5	Chris	Smith	Guard	555-444-3333
	6				
	7				
	8				

Zoom 100%

Click

2

"Phil

		First Name	Last Name	Position	Phone Number
	1	Steve	Poland	Center	555-555-1111
	2	Joe	Bucki	Receiver	555-222-2222
	3	Alex	Anderson	Receiver	555-333-3333
	4	Phil	Poland	Guard	555-444-4444
✓	5	Chris	Smith	Guard	555-444-3333
	6				
	7				
	8				

Zoom 100%

Click

Manually Marking and Unmarking Records in List View

In List view, marking and unmarking records resembles checking and clearing a check box.

1 Click to place a check in the check box to the left of the record number for each record to mark.

2 Click to clear the check in the check box to the left of the record number for each record to unmark.

✓ **Marking or Unmarking All Records**

You can mark or unmark all the records in the database by clicking the small check mark button in the upper-left corner of the database window. In Form view, choose **Record, Unmark All Records** to clear the marking.

Task 33: Showing Only Marked or Unmarked Records

Displaying Marked or Unmarked Records

After you've marked the records you want, you can use that information to control which records appear in either the Form or List view or in printouts. The steps are the same in either view, but this task shows the List view, where listing only selected records is more obvious.

✅ **Hiding Records**

Showing marked or unmarked records is different from hiding a record. Hiding a record means that it doesn't display at all (when you show marked, unmarked, or all records). To hide a record, display it in Form view or click a cell in it in List view. Choose **Record**, **Hide Record**. To redisplay the hidden records in the database, choose **Record**, **Show**, **Hidden Records**.

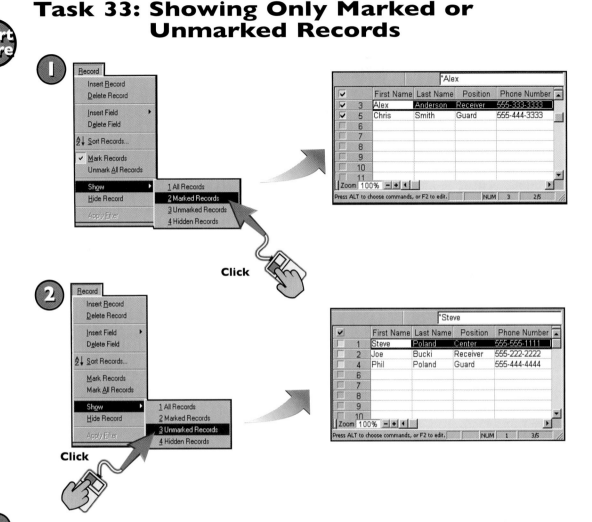

Choose **Record**, **Show**, **Marked Records** to show only the marked records.

Choose **Record**, **Show**, **Unmarked Records** to show only the unmarked records.

Task 34: Redisplaying All Records

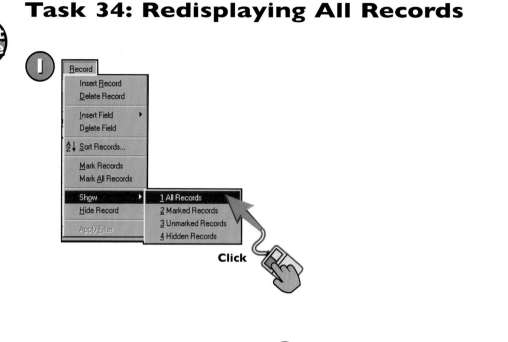

Click

Showing All the Records

When you want to see all the records in your database rather than just marked or unmarked records, you need to redisplay all the records in the database.

① Choose **Record**, **Show**, **All Records**.

② Resume working with the full database of records.

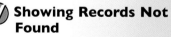

Showing Records Not Found

As noted in the last step of Task 30 after you perform a find, you also need to use the procedure described here to redisplay all the records in the database.

Task 35: Sorting Records

Changing the Order of Records

The database lists your records in the order in which you originally entered them, no matter what type of database you create. However, you can sort the data according to the entries in one or more fields. That is, if you want to reorder the records alphabetically according to last name, you can sort by the Last Name field. If you sort by more than one field, such as the Last Name field and then the First Name field, the database tool first sorts all records by Last Name. If any records have the same entry in the Last Name field, the database tool sorts those records again according to the first name.

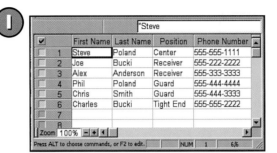

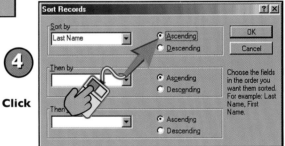

Click

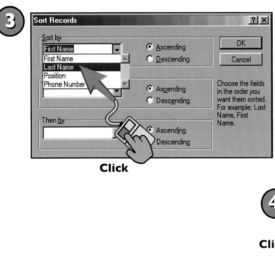

Click

Click

1. Display the database to sort in the view that you want to work with.

2. Choose **Record**, **Sort Records**. (Click **OK** to bypass the First-Time Help window if it appears.)

3. Choose the field to sort by first from the **Sort By** drop-down list.

4. Click **Ascending** or **Descending** to choose the sort order.

5

Sort Records ⑤ [?][x]

Sort by
[Last Name ▼] ○ Ascending [OK]
             ○ Descending [Cancel]

Then by
[_____ ▼] ○ Ascending   Choose the fields
[First Name] ○ Descending in the order you
[Last Name]   want them sorted.
 Position   For example: Last
 Phone Number   Name, First
              ○ Ascending   Name.
              ○ Descending

Click

6

Sort Records [?][x]

Sort by
[Last Name ▼] ○ Ascending [OK]
             ○ Descending [Cancel]

Then by
[First Name ▼] ○ Ascending   Choose the fields
              ○ Descending in the order you
                            want them sorted.
Then by   For example: Last
[_____ ▼] ○ Ascending   Name, First
             ○ Descending   Name.

Click

7

		First Name	Last Name	Position	Phone Number
☑				"Alex	
	1	Alex	Anderson	Receiver	555-333-3333
	2	Charles	Bucki	Tight End	555-555-2222
	3	Joe	Bucki	Receiver	555-222-2222
	4	Phil	Poland	Guard	555-444-4444
	5	Steve	Poland	Center	555-555-1111
	6	Chris	Smith	Guard	555-444-3333
	7				
	8				

Zoom 100% [-][+][◀][ ] [▶]

5 Use the two Then By drop-down lists to specify a second (and third) sort field and sort order, if needed.

6 Click **OK**.

7 View and work with the sorted records.

Choosing a Sort Order

The ascending sort order sorts records in **A-Z** or **1,2,3** order. The descending sort order sorts records in **Z-A** or **3,2,1** order.

✓ **Undoing a Sort**
If you want to undo a sort, choose **Edit, Undo Sort** to do so before you save the file or perform another action. Otherwise, you won't be able to undo the sort. However, if you want to be able to return records to their original order, create a "Record Number" or "ID" field when you create the database, and then enter the number for each record as you create it.

✓ **Creating a Sorted Printout**
Sort your database before you print if you want the records to appear in a particular order in the printout.

Task 36: Inserting a Record

Adding a Record in a Database

Databases grow over time. You can add a new record at the end of the database in the Form view by pressing **Ctrl+End**, typing the new record information (press **Tab** between fields), and pressing **Tab** to finish the record. Or, you can click the first blank row in the List view and enter new record information. However, if you've already sorted the data, you might want to insert the new record at a specific location in the database as described in this task.

✓ Adding a New Field

You also can insert a new field in all of the records. It's easiest to do so in the List view. Right-click the field name beside which you want to add a new field, point to **Insert Field**, and click **Before or After**. Use the Insert Field dialog box to specify a **Field Name** and **Format**, click **Add**, and then **Done**.

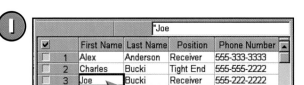

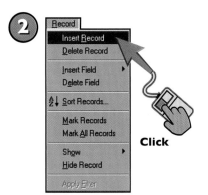

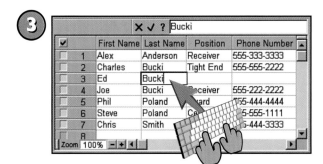

1. Select the record before which you want to insert a new record. (Display the record in Form view or click a cell in it in List view.)

2. Choose **Record**, **Insert Record**.

3. Enter the field contents for the new record.

Task 37: Deleting a Record

Start Here

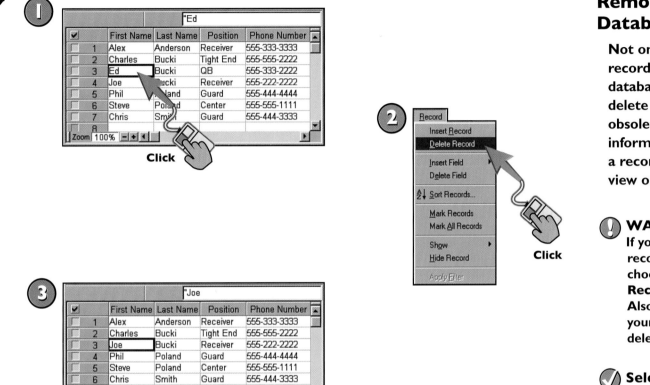

Click

Click

Removing a Database Record

Not only can you add records to update your database, but you can also delete records with obsolete or inaccurate information. You can delete a record in either the **Form** view or the **List** view.

WARNING

If you mistakenly delete a record, immediately choose **Edit, Undo Delete Record** to reinstate it. Also, I recommend saving your database before deleting any records.

Selecting More Than One Record

You can choose multiple contiguous records in **List** view, and then use the **Record, Delete Record** to delete all of them. To select multiple records, click the row (record) number for the first record to delete. Press and hold down the **Shift** key, and click the row number for the last record to delete.

1. Select the record you want to delete. (Display the record in Form view or click a cell in it in List view.)

2. Choose **Record**, **Delete Record**.

3. You can work with the remaining database records.

Displaying Another Works File or Tool

You can create or open as many Works files as you want during a single sitting at your computer. Only one file can be active (or current or selected) at a time, and the current file determines which Works tool's menus and toolbar buttons appear. To switch to another Works tool or Works Suite application, you either have to create a new file or display another file created in a different Works tool or suite application, as described in this task.

 Reopening a File
Use the **File, Open** command in a tool or application to open a Works file that you've previously saved as described in Task 40.

Task 38: Switching Between Open Files (and Tools)

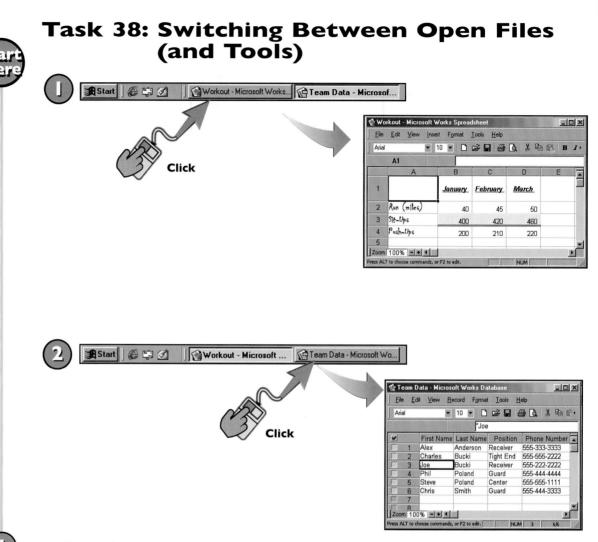

 On the Windows taskbar, click the button for the file and tool or application to display.

② Click another taskbar button when needed to display the file and the applicable Works tool.

Task 39: Printing a File

Start Here

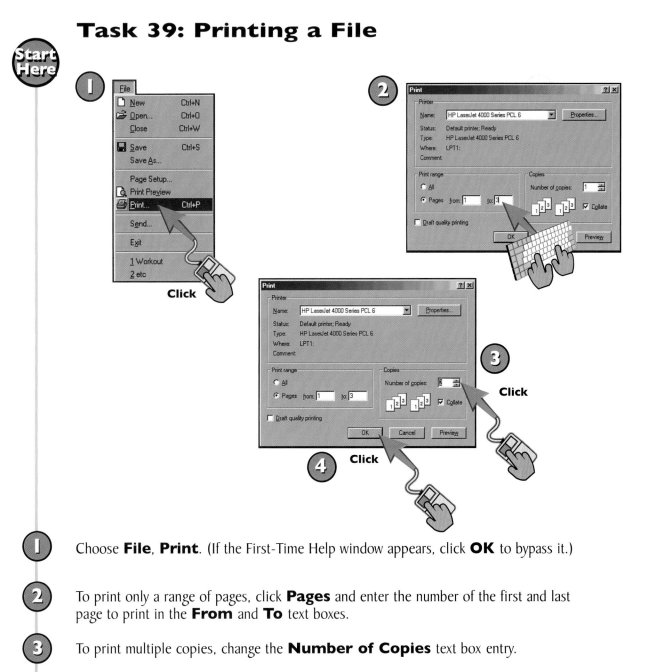

Click

Click

Click

Making a Printout in a Works Tool

No matter which Works tool you're presently using, the process for printing the current file is the same. You can print all the pages in the file or specify a range of pages using the **From** and **To** text boxes. You also can enter a number of copies to print. The only differences appear in what or how you can print. For a spreadsheet, you can choose draft-quality printing to print a draft. For a database, you can print all records or the current record only.

1. Choose **File**, **Print**. (If the First-Time Help window appears, click **OK** to bypass it.)

2. To print only a range of pages, click **Pages** and enter the number of the first and last page to print in the **From** and **To** text boxes.

3. To print multiple copies, change the **Number of Copies** text box entry.

4. Change any other settings and click **OK** to print.

✅ **Printing in a Snap**
To print one copy of the current Works file with the default printing settings, click the **Print** button on the toolbar.

End Task

Task 40: Saving, Closing, and Exiting

Saving and Closing in Works

As in Word, saving a file in a Works tool stores the file to disk so that you can work with it later. After you save a particular file, you can close it so that you can concentrate on working with another Works tool.

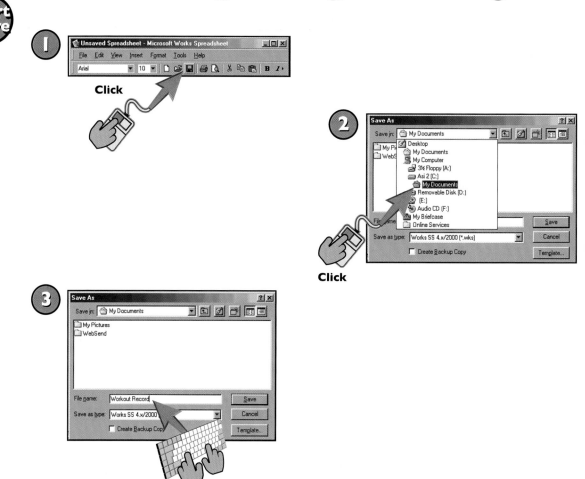

Start Here

Click

Click

 Saving Reminder
If you forget to save a file or your changes to it and try to exit the Works tool or close the file, Works reminds you to save the file.

1 Click the **Save** button on the toolbar.

2 To save to a disk or folder other than the default one, open the **Save In** list and select the folder to use.

3 Click in the **File Name** text box and enter the filename to use.

 Next Step

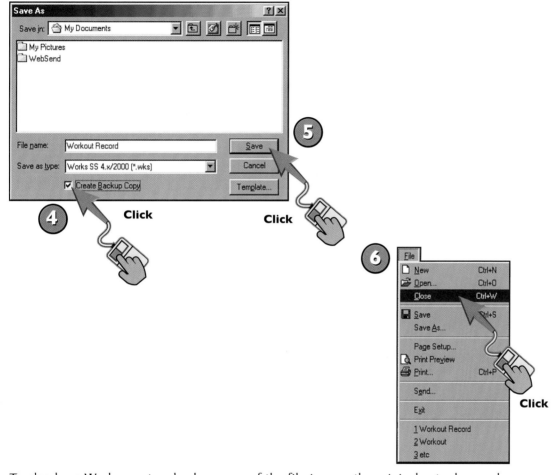

Using Your Backup File

If you accidentally delete your original file or it somehow becomes damaged so that you can't open it, you can open the backup file if you've created one. To do so, choose **File, Open**. Choose **Backup Files (*.b*)** from the Files of Type drop-down list. Use the Look In list if needed to select the disk and folder holding the backup file, click the file when it appears in the dialog box, and click **Open.**

4 To also have Works create a backup copy of the file in case the original gets damaged, check **Create Backup Copy**.

5 Click the **Save** button.

6 Choose **File, Close** to close the file after you've saved it. If no other files are open, this also closes the Works tool.

✓ **Saving for Safety**
After you save your file the first time, you should save it every 10 minutes or so thereafter by clicking the Save button.

Task 41: Starting and Exiting Calendar

Opening Your Calendar from the Task Launcher

Works (Works Suite) now includes a calendar tool. You can use the Works Calendar to track all your family happenings: doctors' appointments, sports practices, birthdays, and more. You can start the calendar tool from the Works Suite Task Launcher, as described in this task.

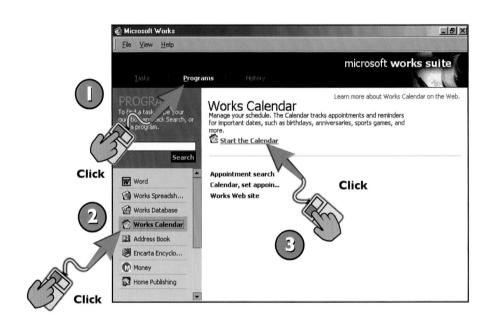

✓ **The Menu Method**
You also can start the Calendar tool from your Windows desktop. Click **Start,** point to **Programs,** point to **Microsoft Works,** and click Microsoft Works **Calendar.**

 On the Task Launcher, click the **Programs** choice.

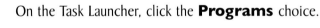 Click **Works Calendar** in the Programs list.

③ Click **Start the Calendar**. (If you are prompted to make Works Calendar your default calendar, click the appropriate choice.)

Leaving the Calendar

Unlike the other Works tools and Works Suite applications, the calendar tool doesn't enable you to create separate files. The upside is that whenever you open Calendar, your schedule information appears. When you close the calendar, you don't have to worry about saving— Calendar takes care of it for you.

Click

④ Close the Works Help window, and create your calendar entries (see Tasks 42 through 49).

⑤ Choose **File, Exit**. Close the Works Task Launcher, if you're finished working.

Task 42: Adding an Appointment

Noting an Upcoming Obligation

The Works Calendar holds your *appointments*—meetings, practices, doctor visits, and other deadlines to meet or events to attend. You can categorize your appointments so that you can list only a particular type of appointment. You can even have the calendar tool remind you of an upcoming event. This task shows you how to add appointments into your calendar.

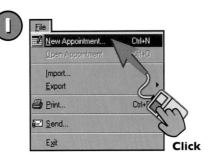

Click

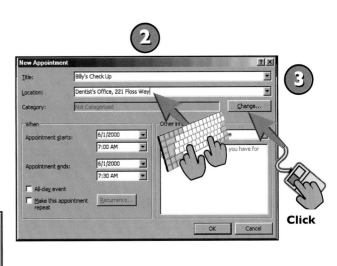

Click

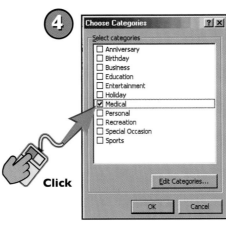

Click

✓ Other Special Days
You use a special method to enter birthdays and holidays into the calendar. Task 46 explains how to enter those special days.

1 Choose **File**, **New Appointment** or click the **New Appointment** button on the toolbar.

2 Enter the **Title** and **Location** for the appointment.

3 Click the **Change** button beside the Category text box.

4 Click the **Category** to apply, and then click **OK**.

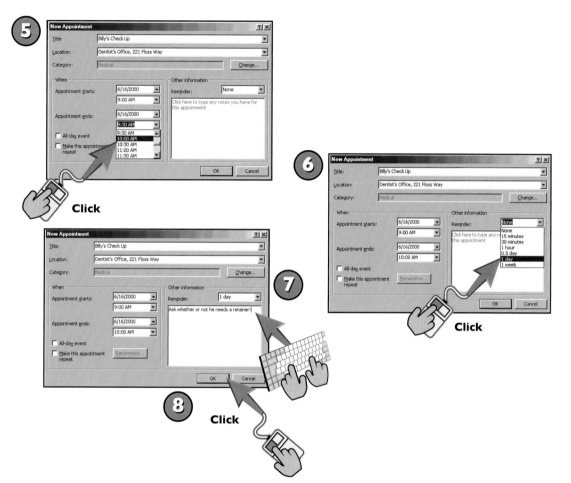

Blocking Out an Entire Day

If you're scheduling an event that will last a full day, such as a family reunion or the date when your family has to travel to another town for a sports tournament, you don't have to mark specific starting and ending appointment times. Instead, click to check the All-Day Event check box in the New Appointment dialog box.

Reminder About Reminders

Unless you use your computer constantly, you should have Calendar display a reminder about your appointment a day or a week in advance. This increases the likelihood that you'll actually turn your computer on to *see* the reminder.

5 Use the Appointment Starts and Appointment Ends drop-down lists to schedule the date and time for the appointment.

6 Make a choice from the Reminder drop-down list if you want Calendar to display and advanced notice about the appointment.

7 Enter any notes you have about the appointment.

8 Click **OK**.

Task 43: Creating a Category

Making Categories You Need

The Works Calendar offers several predefined categories to suit all your family activities, from educational to sports functions. However, you might find that you want to add your own categories, such as a **Workout** category to earmark time you've set aside for your own workouts (as opposed to sports events that you view). This task shows you how easily you can add your own category.

 Delete Alert

Calendar doesn't warn or caution you when you delete a category. If you mistakenly delete a category, immediately click the **Cancel** button to close the Edit Categories dialog box. When you reopen the dialog box, the deleted category will be back in place.

 Start Here

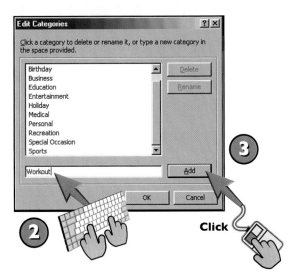

Click

Click

Click

1 Choose **Edit**, **Categories**.

2 Type a name for the new category.

3 Click the **Add** button beside the new category name.

4 After repeating steps 2 and 3 to add other categories, click **OK** to finish.

 End Task

Task 44: Deleting an Appointment

1

Microsoft Works Calendar
File Edit View Help

◀ Previous Day Tuesday, June 13, 2000 Next Day ▶

Click here to add... ◀ June 2000 ▶
S M T W T F S
28 29 30 31 1 2 3
7am 4 5 6 7 8 9 10
8⁰⁰ 11 12 13 14 15 16 17
9⁰⁰ 18 19 20 21 22 23 24
10⁰⁰ 25 26 27 28 29 30 1
2 3 4 5 6 7 8

Click

3

Microsoft Works Calendar
File Edit View Help

Click

2

◀ Previous Day Friday, June 16, 2000 Next Day ▶
Click here to add an all-day event

7am
8⁰⁰
9⁰⁰ Billy's Check Up
10⁰⁰
11⁰⁰
12pm
1⁰⁰ Pick Up Jane from Airport
2⁰⁰
3⁰⁰

Click

4

Works Calendar
❓ Are you sure that you want to permanently delete the selected item?
☑ Always confirm before deleting.
Yes   No

Click

Removing a Scheduled Item

Just as you can erase an item from your paper appointment book, you can remove an appointment you've added into the Works Calendar. To be sure you want to delete the information from your schedule, the calendar tool asks you to confirm the deletion.

✅ **Move It**
To reschedule an appointment, display the date that holds the appointment. Double-click the appointment in the calendar. Make needed changes in the Edit Appointment dialog box, and then click OK.

✅ **Perfect Timing**
To create an appointment for a particular date and time, display the proper date, and double-click the desired time slot.

1 Click the date at the top of the calendar, click an arrow to choose another month, if needed, and then click the desired date.

2 Click the appointment to delete.

3 Click the **Delete** button on the toolbar.

4 Click **Yes** to confirm the deletion.

End Task

Letting Calendar Help with Scheduling

Many events in life occur on a regular basis. Your kids might have weekly music lessons, or you might meet a friend to work out once a month. Rather than going through your schedule and plugging in each and every weekly or monthly appointment, you can tell Calendar to add a recurring (repeating) appointment.

Task 45: Making a Repeating Appointment

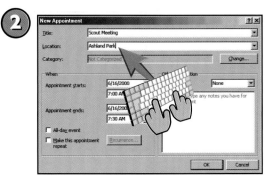

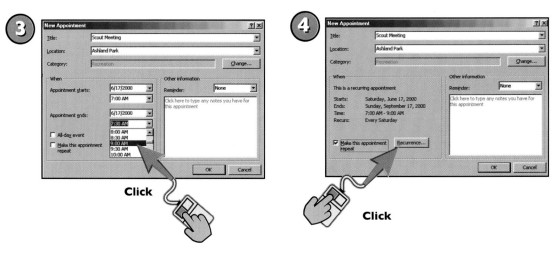

Click

Click

Click

① Choose **File**, **New Appointment**.

② Enter the **Title** and **Location** for the appointment, and assign an appointment category, if desired.

③ Use the Appointment Starts and Appointment Ends drop-down list to specify the first instance of the appointment.

④ Click to check the **Make This Appointment Repeat** check box, and then click the **Recurrence** button.

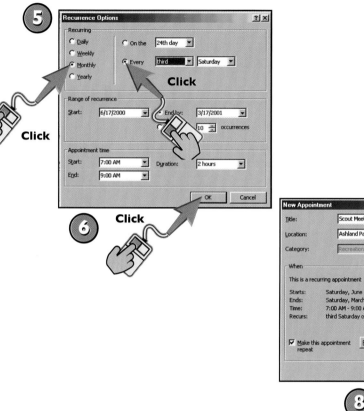

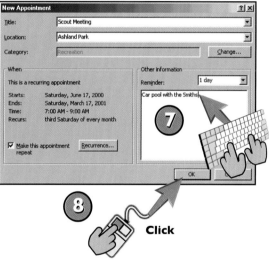

Working with a Recurring Appointment

All the instances that result from a recurring appointment are called a series. If you click one instance of a recurring appointment and then click the **Delete** button, the Delete Appointment dialog box asks you to click either **Delete This Occurrence** (to delete only one instance of the recurring appointment) or **Delete the Series** (to delete them all). Click the appropriate option, and click **OK**. Similarly, if you double-click an instance of a recurring appointment to edit it, you must choose either **Open This Occurrence** or **Open the Series** before clicking **OK**. Depending on your choice, your subsequent changes apply to only one instance of the recurring appointment, or all of them.

5 In the Recurring area of the dialog box, specify how often the appointment recurs by clicking a choice at the left and the appropriate options at the right.

6 Make any other adjustments needed for the recurring appointment information, and click **OK**.

7 Set a reminder and enter appointment notes, if applicable.

8 Click **OK**.

Task 46: Adding Birthdays and Holidays

Marking Holidays

Your holiday schedule will vary based on the country in which you're living and the religion you and your family practice. (Being politically correct, Works doesn't assume that we all live in the U.S. or have the same faith.) So, you have to tell Works which holidays to add in to your calendar.

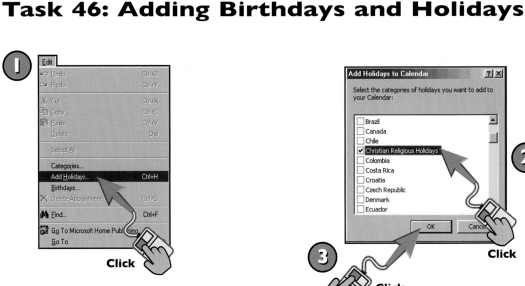

Click

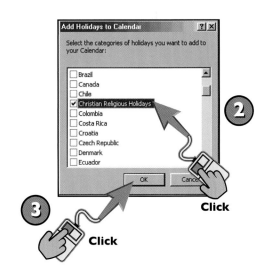

Click

Click

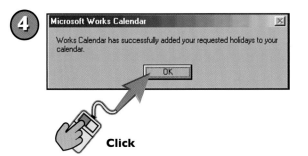

Click

1. Choose **Edit**, **Add Holidays**.

2. To add religious holidays, click the proper choice in the list. For non-United States residents, click the desired country, scroll down, and click to clear the check beside **United States**.

3. Click **OK**.

4. Click **OK** again to confirm the additions.

Adding Contact Birthdays

In Part 4, Task 11, you learn how to add information about a contact into your electronic Address Book for use with e-mail and other Works Suite applications. When you're creating an Address Book entry, you can use the Personal tab in the Properties dialog box for the contact to enter the person's birthday and anniversary. Rather than entering that information all over again in Works Calendar, you can use a simple command to add birthdays and anniversaries from the Address Book into your schedule.

Edit

Undo	Ctrl+Z
Redo	Ctrl+Y
Cut	Ctrl+X
Copy	Ctrl+C
Paste	Ctrl+V
Delete	Del
Select All	
Categories...	
Add Holidays...	Ctrl+H
Birthdays...	
Delete Appointment	Ctrl+D
Find...	Ctrl+F
Go To Microsoft Home Publishing	
Go To	

Click

Works Calendar

Microsoft Works successfully updated the Calendar with birthdays and anniversaries from your address book for the following: 3 events.

OK

☑ Update the Calendar with new birthday and anniversary information from the address book each time you open the Calendar.

Click

5 Choose **Edit**, **Birthdays**.

6 When Works Calendar informs you that it's added the birthday information, click **OK**.

Task 47: Changing the Calendar View

Viewing More Than a Day

The default Works Calendar view shows you the schedule for a single day. You can view a full week's calendar or a full month's calendar, whichever you find more convenient. For example, you can view your weekly calendar on a Sunday to see what you have on your plate for the week to come.

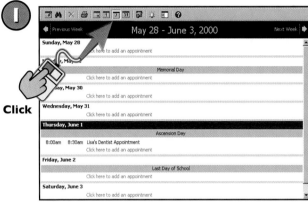

Click

Click

 Hour by Hour
If you switch back to the day view and don't see the hour-by-hour schedule for the day, choose **View**, **Show Day in Hours**.

① Click the **View Week** button on the toolbar.

② Click the **View Month** button on the toolbar.

Next Step

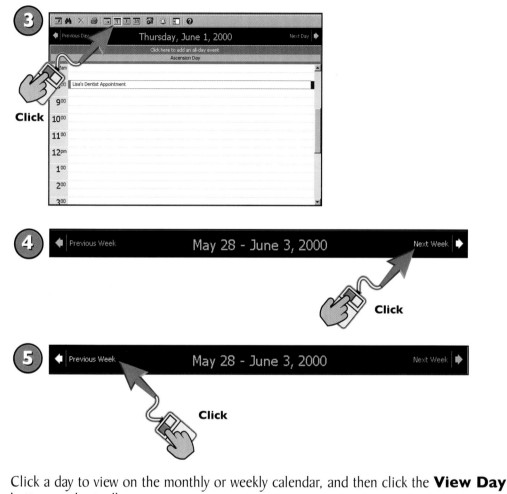

Finding a Date

If you want to jump directly to a particular date no matter what calendar view you're using, choose **Edit, Go To, Date.** Type the desired date in the **Enter Date** text box, and click **OK.**

3 Click a day to view on the monthly or weekly calendar, and then click the **View Day** button on the toolbar.

4 Click the **Next (Interval)** button to scroll the calendar to the next day, week, or month.

5 Click the **Previous (Interval)** button to scroll the calendar to the previous day, week, or month.

Task 48: Dealing with a Reminder

Responding to Appointment Reminders

If you've added a reminder for an appointment, the View Reminders window opens at the reminder time you specified—a day or hour before the appointment, for example. You can then get more information about the reminder. You also can click the **Reminders** button on the Calendar toolbar at any time to view upcoming reminders.

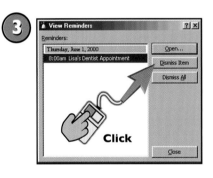

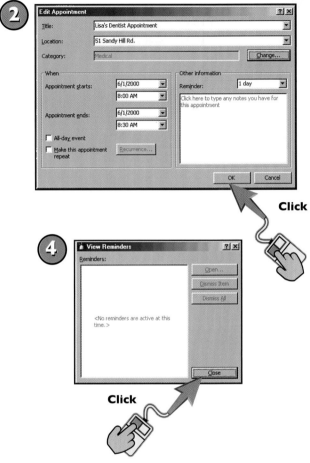

(✓) No Dismissal
If you don't want to dismiss a reminder (so that Calendar will display it again later), click the **Close** button in the View Reminders window without clicking the Dismiss Item or Dismiss All button.

1 If more than one appointment appears, click the one to view, and click the **Open** button to see the details about the appointment.

2 Click **OK** to close the appointment information after you review it.

3 Click the **Dismiss Item** button to close the reminder and tell the Calendar you don't want to see it again.

4 Click **Close** to close the View Reminders window.

Task 49: Printing Your Calendar

①

File
New Appointment...   Ctrl+N
Open Appointment   Ctrl+O

Import...
Export ▶

🖨 Print...   Ctrl+P

📧 Send...

Exit

Click

②

Print   ?×
Style
hours | Day list | Day list by sections | Week | Month - Portrait | Month - Landscape

Click

Range
Start: 2000   End date: 6/17/2000
Start: 8:00 AM   End time: 9:00 PM

June 2000
S M T W T F S
28 29 30 31 1 2 3
4 5 6 7 8 9 10
11 12 13 14 15 16 **17**
18 19 20 21 22 23 24
25 26 27 28 29 30 1
2 3 4 5 6 7 8

Include
⦿ Appointments currently selected in the Category Filter
○ All appointments
☐ Appointment details

OK

③ **Click**

④

Print   ×
Printer
Name: HP LaserJet 4000 Series PCL 6 ▼   Properties
Status: Default printer; Ready
Type: HP LaserJet 4000 Series PCL 6
Where: LPT1:
Comment: ☐ Print to file

Print range
⦿ All
○ Pages from: 1 to: 1
○ Selection

Copies
Number of copies: 1
☐ Collate

Print frames
○ As laid out on screen
○ Only the selected frame
⦿ All frames individually

☐ Print all linked documents   ☐ Print table of links

OK   Cancel

Click

Getting It on Paper

Even if you're using **Works Suite** on a notebook computer, chances are you won't lug it with you all the time, especially if you're doing something such as running family errands on a Saturday or visiting family in another town. So, for "on-the-go" situations, you might want to print a hard copy of your upcoming appointments to tuck into your purse or wallet. You can choose a number of different styles for your printout, depending on how much information you'd like for it to include.

① Choose **File**, **Print**.

② Click the desired printout type in the **Style** area.

③ Specify the **Range** of dates to print and what to include, and then click **OK**.

④ Specify other print options such as the number of copies to print, and click **OK**.

ⓘ WARNING
If you pick a weekly print style, each printed page starts on Monday. So, if you pick a date range that doesn't run from Monday through Sunday, your printout will include more pages than you expected.

Tracking Your Finances with Money 2000 Standard

You can use your home computer to get yourself organized once and for all. One important area of your life that you can organize with a computer is your finances. Part 3 shows you how to use Microsoft Money 2000 to set up a checking account, enter bills and other transactions, print checks, set up a budget, and track investments.

Tasks

Task 1: Starting and Exiting Money

Starting and Closing the Money Program

Financial organizer software tracks money you add to and remove from your bank account, and enables you to enter and print checks and create a budget. Works Suite includes the Money financial organizer software. You can start Money as described here, start it from the Works Suite Task Launcher, or double-click the Microsoft Money icon on your desktop.

✓ Money Setup Help

The first time you start Money, it presents the Money Setup Assistant to help you create a new Money file and accounts in the file. To use the Setup Assistant, insert the Works Suite Disc 2 CD-ROM in your CD-ROM drive and click **Start Here**. Click **Next** to continue or click the **Start Using Money Now** link and follow the prompts to close the Setup Assistant.

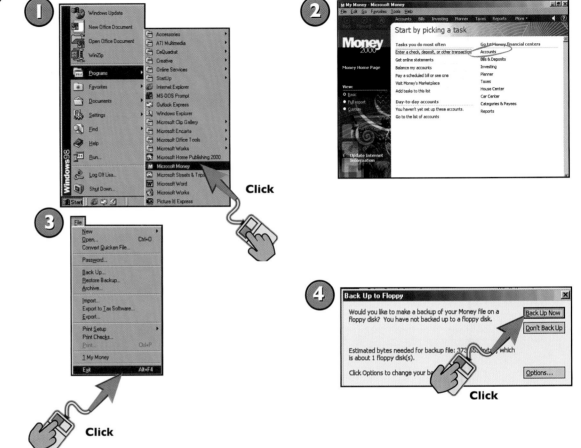

Click

Click

Click

① Click **Start**, **Programs**, **Microsoft Money**.

② When the Money Home Page opens, you can set up your accounts or otherwise work in Money.

③ Choose **File**, **Exit** or press **Alt+F4** when you're ready to exit Money.

④ Insert a floppy disk and click **Back Up Now** in the Back Up to Floppy dialog box if it appears.

Task 2: Creating a Money File

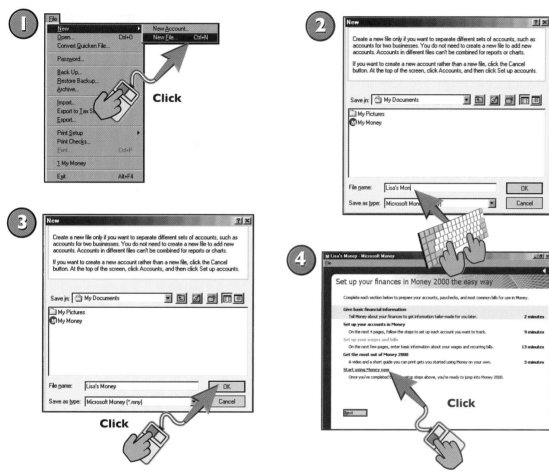

Creating a File for Your Financial Information

Money stores the different types of financial information you enter in a file. If you start the Money program without using the Setup Assistant, Money automatically creates your first file and names the file My Money. If you'll be the only one in your household using Money, start using the My Money file. If more than one person will be using Money and each person's financial information needs to stay separated, then each user needs to create and name his or her own Money file.

✔ **Choosing a Money File**
When you start Money, it opens the file you most recently used (or created). To work with the financial information in a different Money file, you need to open the Money file you want to use. See Task 18 to learn how to open the file of your choice.

---

1 Choose **File**, **New, New File** (**Ctrl+N**).

2 Type the name for the new file in the **File Name** text box.

3 Click **OK**.

4 Use the Setup Assistant, or click the **Start Using Money Now** link and use the prompts to return to Money.

Task 3: Setting Up a Checking Account

Creating Your Checking Account

Within each Money file, you create *accounts* to track your savings, checking, and investment accounts. You enter information about each transaction you perform with that account's funds into the account in Money. When you create a checking account in Money, you can enter a bill *transaction* into that checking account and then print a hard copy (paper) check to pay each bill.

✅ **Displaying the Accounts Center**
You also can display the Accounts Center screen by choosing **Go, Accounts** (**Ctrl+Shift+A**). If you don't see icons for various accounts and buttons for managing accounts but instead see a register for an existing account, click the **Account Manager** button to the right of the account name.

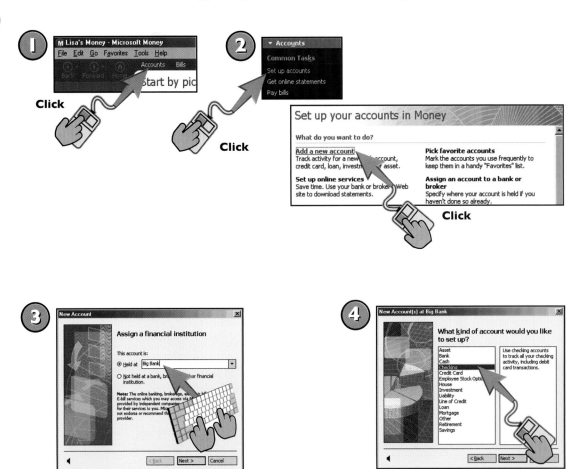

Click

Click

Click

Click

1 Click the **Accounts** link below the menu bar.

2 Click the **Set Up Accounts** link at the left side of the Accounts Center screen; click **Add a New Account**.

3 Enter the name of your bank in the **Held At** text box. Click **Next**. Click the option button for your bank name and **Next**.

4 Leave **Checking** selected in the next dialog box, and then click **Next**.

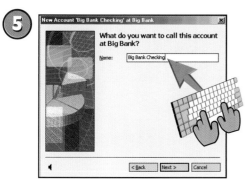

5

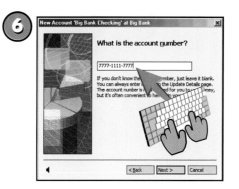

6

Creating a Savings Account

Setting up a savings account is nearly identical to the process described here. Just select a savings account instead of a checking account. An investment account is a bit different, though. Task 15, explains how to set up an account to track your mutual fund or stock investments.

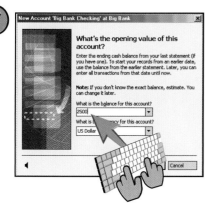

7

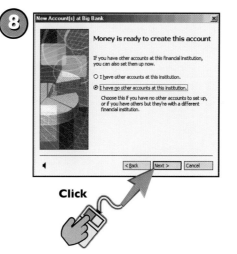

8

Click

5 Edit the suggested account name, if needed, and click **Next**.

6 Enter the account number and click **Next**.

7 Enter the account balance and click **Next**.

8 At the next dialog box, leave the bottom option button selected and click **Next**, **Finish**, and the **Done** button.

⚠ WARNING
You need to be sure to synchronize the checking account balance you enter in Money when you create the account with the balance of your real account with your bank. To do so, work from your most recent, balanced checking account statement from your bank.

End Task

Making Categories to Identify Income and Expenses

To master your budget, you need to understand where your money comes from and where it goes. In Money, you assign a *category* and *subcategory* to each transaction to identify how you made or spent the money involved. You can then use Money to generate reports totaling money you made (or spent) in each category or subcategory. Money offers predefined categories and subcategories. For example, it offers a *Household* category, which contains a *Furnishings* subcategory. You can add your own category or subcategory to supplement the list, such as if you want a *Repairs* subcategory for the *Household* category.

Task 4: Creating Categories and Subcategories

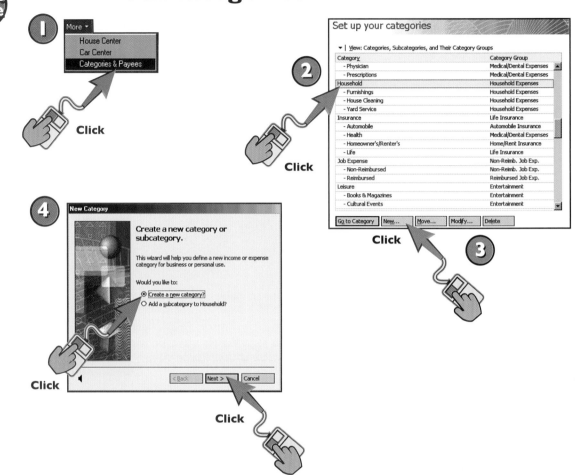

Click the **More** link at the top of any screen, and then click **Categories & Payees** in the menu that opens.

To create a new subcategory, click a category in the lists. Otherwise, don't click anything.

Click the **New** button at the bottom of the Categories & Payees screen.

Select **Create a New Category** or **Add a Subcategory to (Category)** to create either a category or subcategory. Click **Next**.

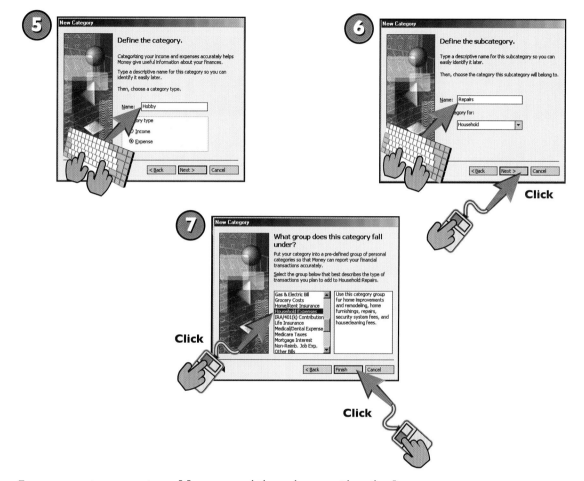

Classifying Categories

Classifications and groups collect categories and subcategories and provide further reporting effectiveness. For example, you might want to assign the **Household Expenses** group to the Food category, selected subcategories in the Bills and Insurance categories, and the Household category. Or, if you have more than one car, you might want to set up a classification for each to accurately assign *Automobile* and *Insurance* expenses for each.

✓ Creating a Report
To display a report after you've entered some transactions (see Tasks 6–10), click the **Reports** link at the top of the screen and click a report category in the list at the left side of the screen. Click the report you want in the Pick a Report or Chart list and click the **Go to Report/Chart** button at the bottom of the screen.

5 For a new category, enter a **Name**, and then choose either the **Income or Expense** option button.

6 For a subcategory, enter the **Name**. Click **Next**.

7 Click the group to assign to the category in the left list, and then click **Finish**.

Accessing Account Information

When you're ready to enter transactions into or otherwise work with an account, you need to return to the list of accounts and select the account with which you want to work. Then, you need to view information about—and information stored in—the account.

✅ **Understanding Transaction Forms**

You enter checks, deposits, transfers, withdrawals, and cash machine (ATM) transactions in the transaction forms, which look like a series of tabs at the bottom of the transaction register. If you don't see the transaction forms when you display the register, click the **View** drop-down list arrow below the account name and click **Transaction Forms** in the menu that appears.

Task 5: Viewing Accounts and Opening an Account

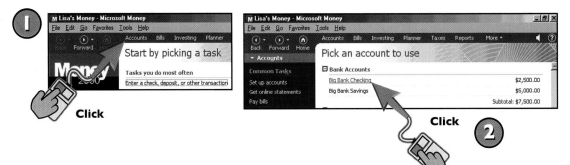

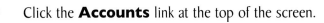

1. Click the **Accounts** link at the top of the screen.

2. To view the transaction register for the account you want to use, click the account's link.

3. Click **Change Account Details** in the list at the left.

4. Change account information as needed in the Update Details screen, and then click **Back**.

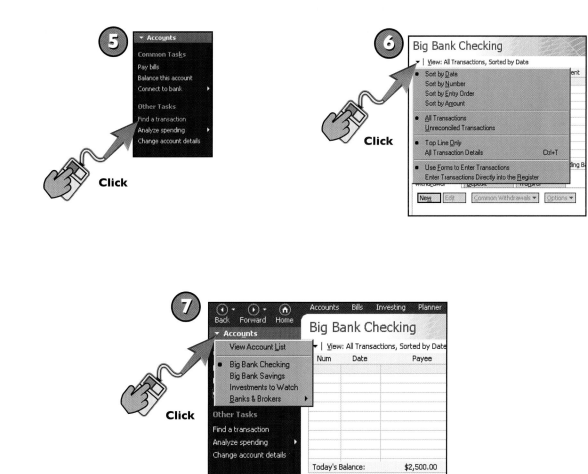

Changing the Account Name

To change the Account Name, click the **Rename** button on the Update Details screen. In the **Modify Account** dialog box that appears, enter a new account name in the **New Name** text box. You also can change the account type by choosing an option button in the Account Type area of the dialog box. Changing account types can really mess up previously entered transactions; for example, if you've entered bills (checks) in a bank account, you don't want to change it to a credit card account. After you finish making your changes in the Modify Account dialog box, click **OK** to close it.

✅ **On the Go**
You also can use the **Go** menu to display your list of accounts, categories, and other financial lists and centers in Money.

5 Click **Find a Transaction** to display the Find and Replace dialog box for finding transactions.

6 Click the **View** drop-down list button and then click a menu choice to sort or filter the list of transactions.

7 Click the **Accounts** drop-down list button at the left to display the list of accounts. Click another account to open it.

Task 6: Entering a Bill (Check)

Writing a Check in Money

Once or twice a month, you sit down with your checkbook and bills, write out checks (bill payments) longhand, and write a corresponding transaction in your paper checkbook register. When you enter a check (bill) in Money and then use Money to print the check, you have to enter the transaction only once. Money records the check in the account register and correctly calculates the new account balance (the amount of money you have left after deducting the check). See Task 11 to learn how to print your checks.

✓ Getting the Numbers Right

When you enter a check (bill) in the checking account register, be sure you enter the correct check number. By default, Money numbers the first check #1001.

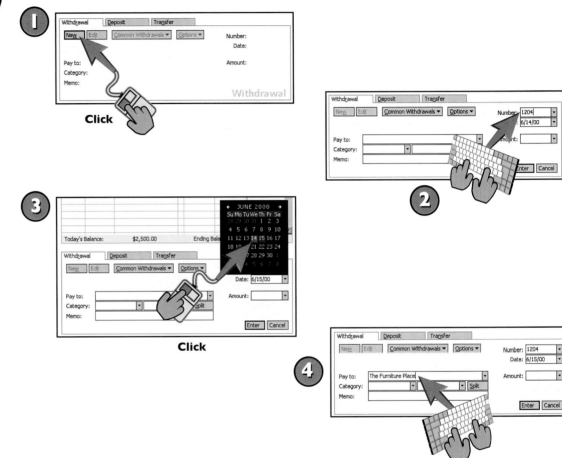

Start Here

Click

Click

1. In the register for the checking account you want to use, click the **Withdrawal** transaction form tab and click **New**.

2. Edit the check number in the **Number** text box, if needed, and press **Tab**.

3. Click the drop-down list arrow beside the **Date** text box, click the date for the check in the calendar that appears, and press **Tab**.

4. Enter a payee in the **Pay To** text box and press **Tab**.

Next Step

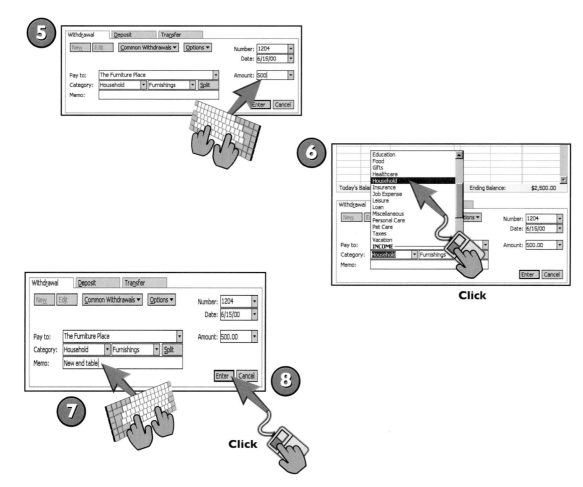

Remembering Payees

After you enter a payee the first time, **Money** stores the payee name and transaction information in its payees list. Then, when you type the first few characters of the payee name in the **Pay To** text box, the rest of the name appears, and you can press **Tab**. (This feature is called *AutoComplete*.) You can then simply edit the Amount, Category, and Memo entries as needed.

✓ **Category, Please**
Based on the name of the payee you enter, Money might suggest a category and subcategory for you, as demonstrated in this task.

✓ **Writing Another Check**
After you enter the first check, click the **New** button on the **Withdrawal** tab to begin entering the next check.

Click

Click

5. Enter the check amount in the **Amount** text box and press **Tab**.

6. Use the left and right Category drop-down lists to assign or change the category and subcategory.

7. Press **Tab** twice, and enter a description or note in the **Memo** text box.

8. Click the **Enter** button on the Withdrawal tab to add the check to the register.

Task 7: Entering a Deposit

Adding a Deposit Transaction

At some point, you'll need to deposit money into your checking account at your bank and record that transaction in your checking account in Money. Similarly, if you receive an electronic payment, such as an automatic payroll deposit or interest payment, you need to enter the deposit in your Money checking account. Money calculates the new balance, so you'll know how much you have available for further checks.

✓ Entering Similar Transactions

The steps described here for making a deposit into a checking account also work for a savings or cash account. Enter the account you want to make a deposit into, display the register for that account, and click the **Deposit** transaction form tab to make the deposit.

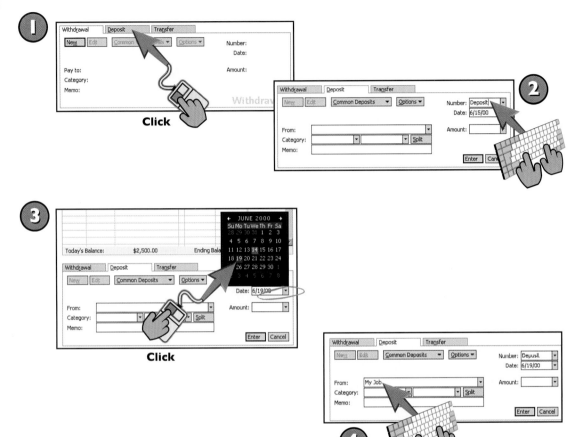

Click

Click

(1) In the register for the account you want to use, click the **Deposit** transaction form tab.

(2) Edit a notation such as **Deposit** in the **Number** text box, if needed. Press **Tab**.

(3) Click the **Date** drop-down list arrow, click the date you made the deposit or the expected electronic deposit date, and press **Tab**.

(4) Enter a payer in the **From** text box, and press **Tab**.

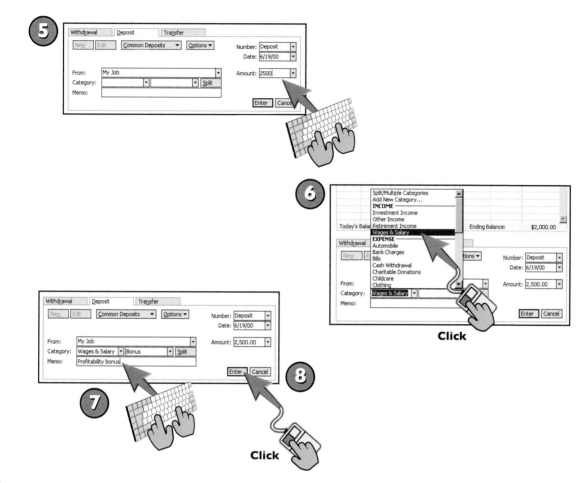

Keeping Deposits Up to Date

Resist the temptation to wait until you receive your monthly statement to enter deposits and instead enter them when you make them. Money will let you overdraft your checking account so that it shows a negative balance. So, if you haven't entered your deposits, you'll have to remember how much you deposited and not exceed that amount when you write checks. This makes you vulnerable to real overdrafts if you make a mistake. Entering the deposits as you make them prevents such a situation.

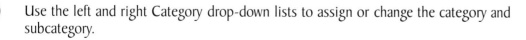

(5) Enter the deposit amount in the **Amount** text box.

(6) Use the left and right Category drop-down lists to assign or change the category and subcategory.

(7) Press **Tab** twice, and enter a description or note in the **Memo** text box.

(8) Click the **Enter** button on the Deposit tab to add the deposit to the register.

⚠ WARNING
Be sure you assign an Income category, not an Expense category, to deposits.

Task 8: Entering a Transfer

Transferring Money Between Accounts

At many banks, you earn more interest in a savings account than a checking account. To maximize your interest returns, keep as much money in savings and as little in checking as possible. This likely means you'll need to transfer money between the accounts, such as transferring part of a paycheck deposited into your checking account to your savings account. As with other transaction types, after you make the real transaction at your bank, enter the transfer in your Money file. Money then calculates the new account balances.

✔ **Keeping It Simple**
Although you could enter a transfer as two separate transactions—a withdrawal from one account and a deposit into another—you can accomplish the feat faster by entering a single transfer transaction.

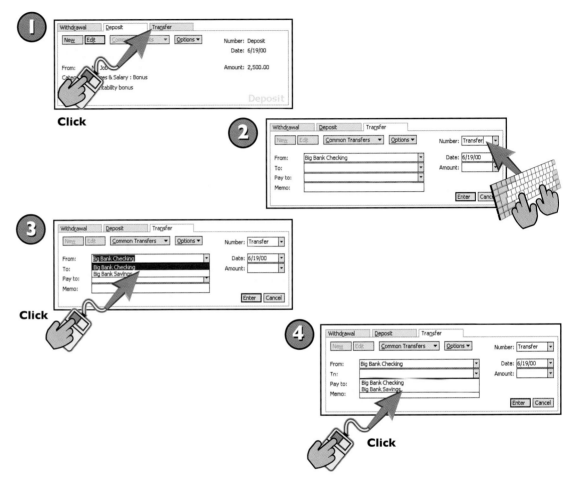

Click

Click

Click

1 In the register for either account, click the **Transfer** transaction form tab.

2 Edit a notation such as **Transfer** in the **Number** text box, if needed. Press **Tab**.

3 Open the From drop-down list and click the account out of which you want to transfer funds, if that account isn't already named.

4 Click the **To** drop-down list arrow and click the account into which you want to transfer funds.

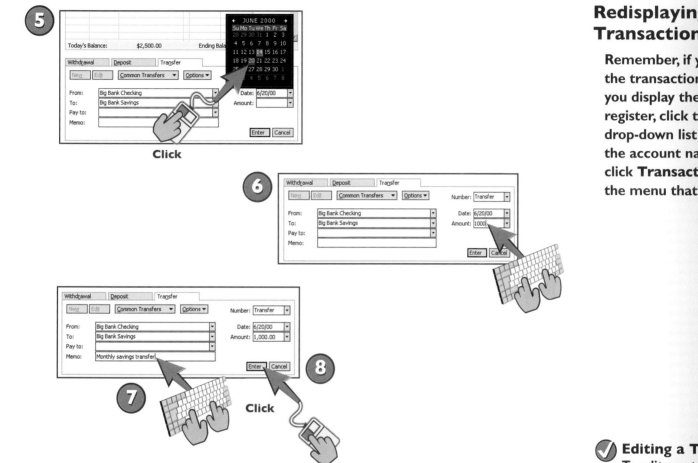

Redisplaying the Transaction Forms

Remember, if you don't see the transaction forms when you display the account register, click the **View** drop-down list arrow below the account name, and then click **Transaction Forms** in the menu that appears.

5 Click the **Date** drop-down list arrow, click the date you made the transfer, and then press **Tab** twice.

6 Enter the transfer amount in the **Amount** text box.

7 Press **Tab** twice and enter a description or note in the **Memo** text box.

8 Click the **Enter** button on the Transfer tab to enter a transaction in the register for each of the accounts.

✔ **Editing a Transaction**
To edit any transaction, double-click it in the register. Make the changes you want in the text boxes on the selected transaction form tab at the bottom of the register, and then click the **Enter** button to accept the changes.

Task 9: Entering a Withdrawal

Recording a Withdrawal

When you withdraw money from your bank using a withdrawal slip, use an **ATM** machine, or even use your debit card, you should enter that transaction as a withdrawal in your checking account (or savings account). When you enter the withdrawal, you can assign a category and subcategory to identify how you spent the money, or even a specific payee, if applicable.

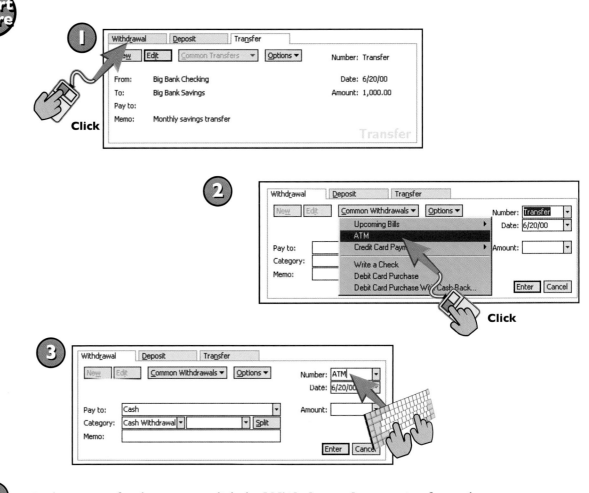

✓ **Recording Bank Fees**
You can enter any extra bank fees charged to your account, such as stop payment fees or **ATM** fees, as withdrawals.

(1) In the register for the account, click the **Withdrawal** transaction form tab.

(2) Click the **Common Withdrawals** button, and then click a withdrawal type.

(3) Make a notation such as **ATM** in the **Number** text box.

④

Withdrawal	Deposit	Transfer

New　Edit　Common Withdrawals ▼　Options ▼　Number: ATM ▼
　　　　　　　　　　　　　　　　　　　　　Date: 6/20/00 ▼

Pay to: Cash ▼　　　Amount: 50| ▼
Category: Cash Withdrawal ▼ | ▼ | Split
Memo:

Enter

⑤

Withdrawal	Deposit	Transfer

New　Edit　Common Withdrawals ▼　Options ▼　Number: ATM ▼
　　　　　　　　　　　　　　　　　　　　　Date: 6/20/00 ▼

Pay to: Cash ▼　　　Amount: 50.00 ▼
Category: Leisure ▼ | ▼ | Split
Memo: Movie and putt-putt

Enter　Cancel

Click

④ Specify the rest of the transaction information.

⑤ Click the **Enter** button on the Withdrawal tab to enter the transaction in the account register.

Splitting a Transaction

What do you do if you withdraw $50 from the bank machine and spend $20 on personal care items from the drugstore and $30 on going to a movie (leisure)? To assign more than one category to a transaction, use the Split button beside the Category drop-down lists on the transaction form. On each line in the Transaction with Multiple Categories window, select the proper Category and subcategory and enter a Description and Amount. Click the Done button when you finish specifying the categories.

✓ **Other Common Transactions**
The Deposit and Transfer forms offer the Common Deposits and Common Transfers buttons, respectively, which you can use to start off other types of transactions.

End Task

Task 10: Printing Checks

Having Money Print Your Checks

While you probably won't cart your computer and printer with you so you can print checks while shopping, you may very well want to use Money 2000 to print checks to pay bills. In Money, you specify which checks to print (using the Number text box), choose a check format, and send the checks to the printer.

Start Here

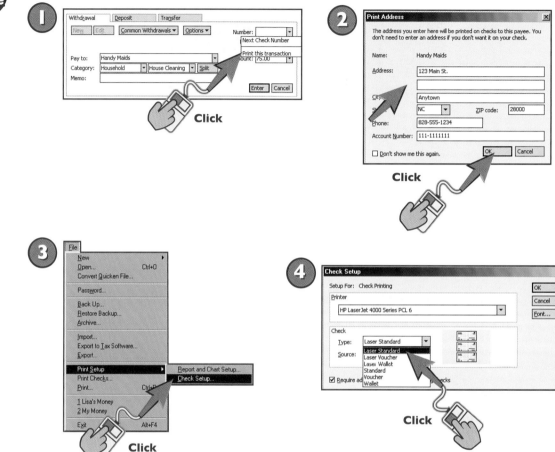

Click

✓ **Editing a Check Transaction**
To edit a check, double-click the check transaction in the checking account register. In the Check transaction form tab, make the changes you want, and then click the **Enter** button.

① For each check to print, select **Print This Transaction** from the Number drop-down list while entering or editing the check.

② After you click **Enter** to finish the check transaction, enter address information for the payee, and click **OK**.

③ Choose **File**, **Print Setup**, **Check Setup**.

④ Verify that the correct printer is selected, choose a check format from the Type drop-down list, and click **OK**.

Next Step

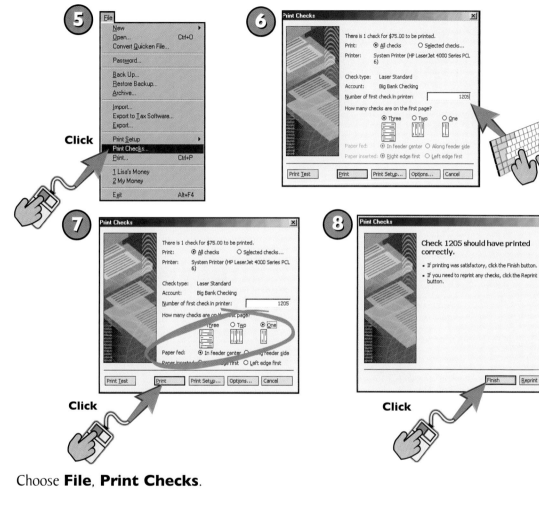

Getting Your Checks

To print your checks from Money 2000, you have to order special checks that work with your printer and have your account and bank information on them. Choose the Help, Ordering Checks command in Money to learn how to order checks. Load the checks into your printer before you begin the print process.

✓ Checking Your Options

Different options appear below the **Number of First Check in Printer** text box of the **Print Checks** dialog box. Change the settings depending on how many checks you're inserting into the printer, and so forth. To test your settings, insert a blank page into the printer, click **Print Test**, and then compare the results with your check format.

5 Choose **File**, **Print Checks**.

6 Leave **All Checks** selected edit the entry in the **Number of First Check in Printer** text box to match the first check you've placed in the printer.

7 Review and correct the other options as needed, and click **Print**.

8 Be sure your checks printed correctly, and click **Finish**.

Reconciling Your Checking Transactions

You have to synchronize your bank records and your Money 2000 checking or savings account register. This process is called *reconciling* or balancing your checkbook (checking account). As soon as possible after you get your monthly bank statement, follow the reconciliation process described here.

✓ Reconciling Other Accounts

You use the same basic steps as those described here to reconcile accounts other than checking accounts.

✓ Identifying Cleared Transactions

After you reconcile the account, cleared transactions display an R in the C column, and the lower-left corner of the register screen displays the date you last balanced the account.

Task 11: Reconciling the Checking Account

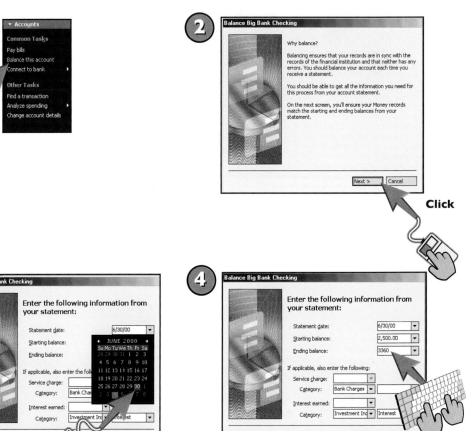

Start Here

Click

Click

Click

With the checking account to reconcile open onscreen, click the **Balance This Account** choice at the left.

Click **Next** in the Balance (Account) dialog box that appears.

Specify the statement date using the **Statement Date** drop-down list.

Verify that the **Starting Balance** matches the statement starting balance. Enter the statement ending balance in the **Ending Balance** text box.

Next Step

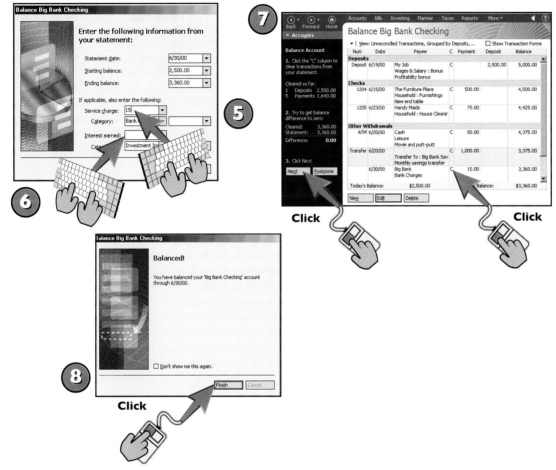

Managing Service Charges

Although you could use the Service Charge text box and Category drop-down list to enter a fee charged for a cash machine (ATM) transaction, this works only if you have only one such fee (or take the time to manually total those fees). It also precludes you from entering the account service charge as you balance the account. It's a better bet to enter each cash machine transaction fee as a separate transaction in the register before you begin balancing the account.

Enter any service charge listed on the statement in the **Service Charge** text box. Optionally, choose a subcategory from the right Category drop-down list.

Enter any interest listed on the statement in the **Interest** text box, and click **Next**.

To clear each transaction on the statement, click to place a C in the **C** column. When the Balance Difference at the left reaches 0, click **Next**.

Click **Finish** at the dialog box that informs you you've balanced your account.

Entering a Transaction That Repeats

Creating *recurring transactions* helps you anticipate and remember when payments are due so you don't mistakenly forget to make one of those payments. A recurring transaction repeats at specified intervals. You use the **Pay Bills** screen to enter and view recurring transactions.

✓ Creating Other Recurring Transactions

You also can create recurring deposit, transfer, or investment purchase transactions by selecting the appropriate transaction type from the **Create New Scheduled Transaction** dialog box, and then clicking **Next** and supplying the transaction information.

Task 12: Creating a Recurring Transaction

Click

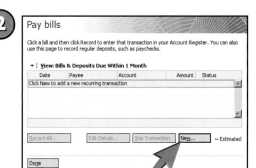

Click

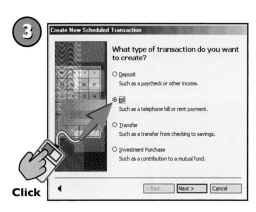

Click

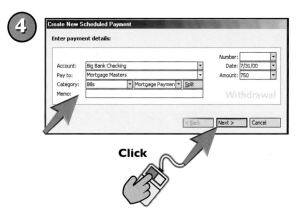

Click

1. Click the **Bills** link at the top of the screen.

2. Click the **New** button on the Pay Bills screen.

3. Click the option button for the transaction type you want (**Bill** in this case), and click **Next**.

4. Choose the **Account** for the recurring transaction, fill in the other information about the transaction, and then click **Next**.

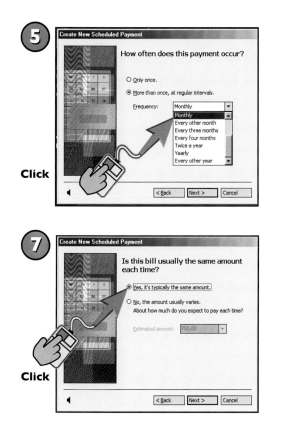

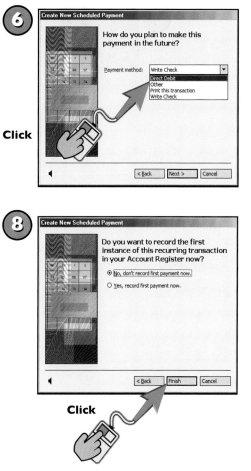

Using the Recurring Transaction

By default, the Microsoft Money Express bill reminder opens when you start your computer. (You also can start it by double-clicking its icon in the system tray.) The Upcoming Bills and Deposits area of the Money Express window lists recurring transactions scheduled to happen within the next 10 days. Click the link for a recurring transaction to display the Record Payment window. Verify and adjust the transaction information, if needed, and click the **Record Payment** button to add the transaction to your account register. Or, if you've already started Money, click the **Bills** link at the top of the screen. Click an upcoming transaction in the Pay Bills screen, and then click the **Record Payment** button to display the record payment window.

(5) Specify how often the payment occurs using the Frequency drop-down list, and then click **Next**.

(6) Specify a **Payment Method**, and then click **Next**.

(7) Click the top option button for payments that don't change or enter an **Estimated Amount**. Click **Next**.

(8) Specify whether or not to record the first payment, and then click **Finish**.

Task 13: Figuring Your Budget

Budgeting Your Money

Entering payments and other transactions means looking back or dealing with the present. To look ahead, you can use Money to calculate a budget, so you'll know how your income stacks up against your expenses. Unlike other budget software, Money includes a category for savings expenditures so you remember to pay yourself (save for the future) before you blow your spare change.

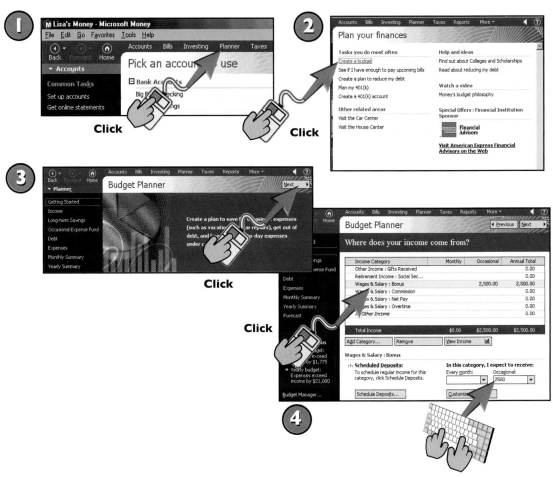

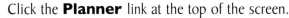

✅ Getting a Head Start

If you've already entered recurring transactions, that information will be reflected in the initial budget values that appear in the Budget Planner screen.

✅ Debt Planning

If you choose the Debt choice at the left side of the Budget Planner screen, you need to click the **Debt Reduction Planner** link to continue.

① Click the **Planner** link at the top of the screen.

② Click the **Create a Budget** link.

③ Click **Next** from the Getting Started page of the Budget Planner to display the Income information.

④ Click each Income Category line, and then enter amounts in the **Every Month** and **Occasional** text boxes.

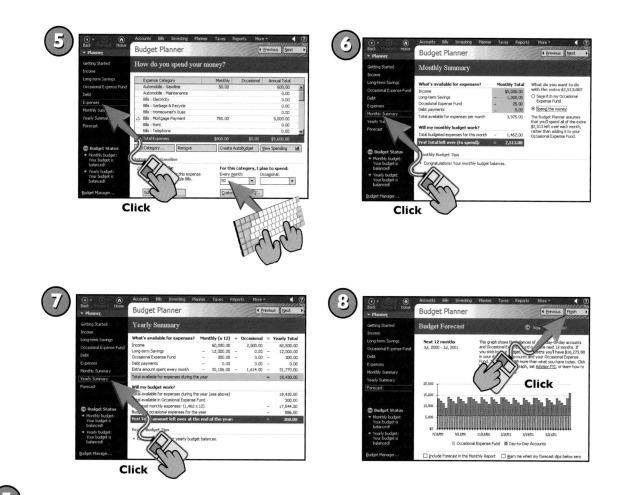

⑤

Budget Planner

How do you spend your money?

Expense Category	Monthly	Occasional	Annual Total
Automobile : Gasoline	50.00		600.00
Automobile : Maintenance			0.00
Bills : Electricity			0.00
Bills : Garbage & Recycle			0.00
Bills : Homeowner's Dues			0.00
Bills : Mortgage Payment	750.00		9,000.00
Bills : Rent			0.00
Bills : Telephone			0.00
Total Expenses	$800.00	$0.00	$9,600.00

Click

⑥

Budget Planner

Monthly Summary

What's available for expenses?	Monthly Total
Income	$5,000.00
Long-term Savings	1,000.00
Occasional Expense Fund	25.00
Debt payments	0.00
Total available for expenses per month	3,975.00

Will my monthly budget work?
Total budgeted expenses for this month − 1,462.00
Yes! Total left over (to spend): = 2,513.00

Click

⑦

Budget Planner

Yearly Summary

What's available for expenses?	Monthly (x 12)	+ Occasional	= Yearly Total
Income	60,000.00	2,500.00	62,500.00
Long-term Savings	− 12,000.00 −	0.00 −	12,000.00
Occasional Expense Fund	− 300.00 −	0.00 −	300.00
Debt payments	− 0.00 −	0.00 −	0.00
Extra amount spent every month	− 30,156.00 −	1,614.00 −	31,770.00
Total available for expenses during the year		=	18,430.00

Click

⑧

Budget Planner

Budget Forecast

Next 12 months
Jul, 2000 – Jul, 2001

Click

☐ Include Forecast in the Monthly Report ☐ Warn me when my forecast dips below zero

AutoBudgeting

If you've entered your income and expenses in the account register for some time and have been diligent about categorizing them, you can use the AutoBudget feature to generate a budget for you. To do so, click the **Expenses** choice at the left side of the **Budget Planner** screen. Click the **Create AutoBudget** button below the list of categories.

Redisplaying Your Budget
The information you enter in the Budget Planner screen stays there until you delete it or change it. To redisplay that budget information at any time, click the **Planner** link at the top of the screen, and then click the **Update My Budget** link.

⑤ In turn, click the **Long-Term Savings**, **Occasional Expense Fund**, and **Expenses** choices at the left, and enter information in the page that appears.

⑥ Click the **Monthly Summary** choice to display a summary.

⑦ Click the **Yearly Summary** choice to display an annualized summary.

⑧ Click the **Forecast** choice to see how your income and expenses might balance out for the coming calendar year, and then click **Finish**.

Task 14: Setting Up an Investment Account

Creating an Account to Track Investments

Just as you create a separate Money 2000 account for each checking or savings account you have, you need to create a separate Money account for each mutual fund or stock investment account you have. Because you have to track some different information when you track investments, such as tracking share prices and dividends, the process for setting up an investment account differs a bit from the process described in Task 3.

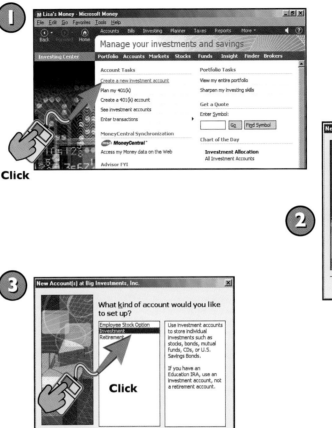

Click

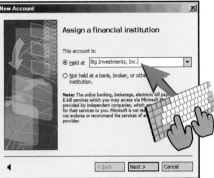

✓ Setting Up Numerous Accounts

The best rule of thumb is to create one investment account for each paper investment account statement you receive each month. That way, you can more clearly track your gains and losses in each account, providing helpful information at tax time.

(1) Click the **Investing** link at the top of the screen, and then click the **Create a New Investment Account** link.

(2) Enter the financial institution name in the **Held At** text box, and click **Next**.

(3) Choose the proper account type from the left list, and click **Next**.

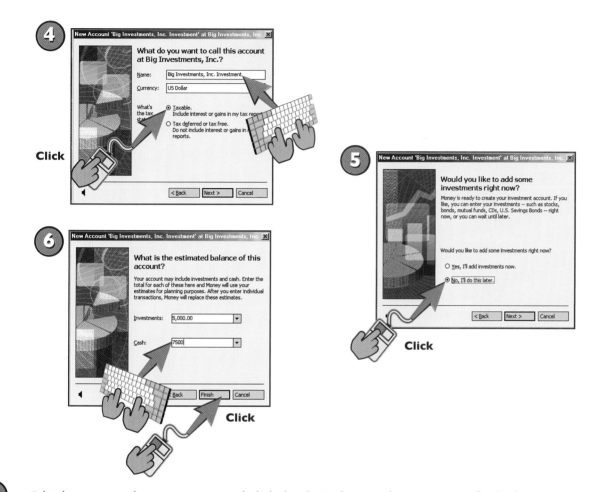

Clarifying Your Initial Entries

If you're starting an investment account from scratch (that is, you've deposited cash in it, but haven't placed any securities trades), enter zero as the estimated investment value and the amount of deposited cash as the current cash value.

✔ Adding Your Account Number

Money doesn't prompt you to enter an account number when you create the investment account, but you can add it later. Click the **Accounts** link at the top of the screen, click the link for the account in the **Pick an Account to Use** list, and click **Change Account Details**. Enter the number in the **Account Number** text box, as well as entering any other details you'd like, and then click the account name choice at the left to work with the account register.

---

4 Edit the suggested account name and click the desired option button to specify whether the investment is tax deferred, and then click **Next**.

5 Click the **No, I'll Do This Later** option button and then **Next**.

6 Enter the estimated value of investments and cash already in the account, and click **Finish**.

Task 15: Adding a Stock or Mutual Fund Buy to the Account

Entering an Investment Purchase

Each time you buy or sell stock, mutual fund shares, or other investments, or receive a dividend or other distribution that's deposited into your investment account, it's a transaction. You need to enter each transaction into the register for the investment account in Money 2000. Entering an investment account transaction resembles doing so in a checking account as you've seen before, but you need to provide even more information, as described in this task.

✅ **Entering Other Types of Investments**
This task shows a stock purchase. Obviously, you'll want to choose the right Investment type (stock, mutual fund, and so on) and Activity (Buy, Sell, Dividend deposit, and so on) for each of your transactions.

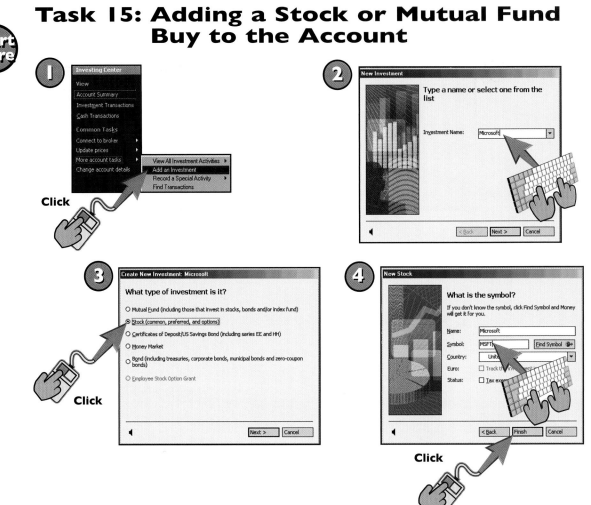

Start Here

Click

Click

Click

① With the investment account open, click the **More Account Tasks** choice at the left, and then click **Add an Investment**.

② Enter the name of the stock or mutual fund in the **Investment Name** text box, and click **Next**.

③ Click the option button for the investment type, and then click **Next**.

④ Specify the stock ticker **Symbol** and **Status**. Click **Finish**.

Next Step

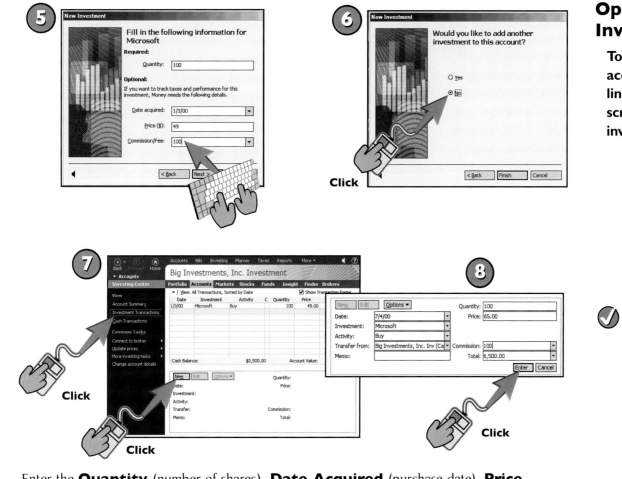

Opening the Investment Account

To open your investment account, click the **Accounts** link near the top of the screen. Click the link for the investment account name.

✓ **Moving Between Cash and Investments**
When your brokerage account stores both investments and cash, Money tracks the cash portion of the account in a separate register linked to the main investment account. To move to the register tracking cash, click **Cash Transactions** at the left side of the main investment account register. To return to the register for the main account, click **Investment Transactions**.

⑤ Enter the **Quantity** (number of shares), **Date Acquired** (purchase date), **Price** (per share or unit), and **Commission/Fee** (broker's fee amount). Click **Next**.

⑥ Leave **No** selected, and then click **Finish**.

⑦ To add other transactions, click the **Investment Transactions** choice at the left, and then click the **New** button.

⑧ Enter transaction information, and then click the **Enter** button on the transaction form to enter the transaction.

End Task

Task 16: Backing Up Your Money File

Creating a Backup Money File

Money 2000 automatically asks you whether you want to back up the open file when you exit Money. However, that doesn't prevent you from losing information if there's a power fluctuation that reboots your computer without warning, or if some other catastrophe occurs. Back up the Money file you're working with every 10 minutes or so.

✓ Using the Backup File

Backing up saves a copy of the Money file with exactly the information it held when you completed the backup process. If your current file won't open and you need to use that backup data, choose **File, Restore Backup**. Leave Restore from a Backup file selected and click **Next**. If the file to restore appears under the Restore from Default Backup file listed in the Restore Backup dialog box, click **Restore** twice.

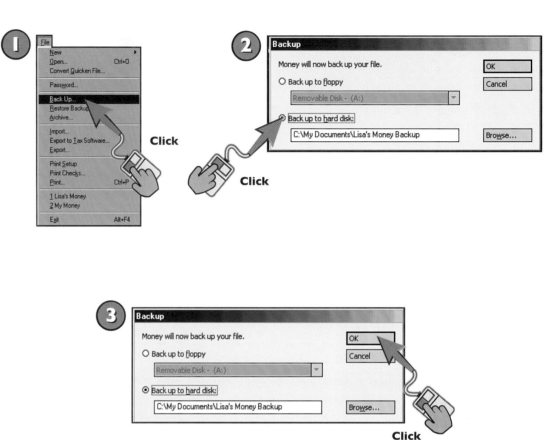

Start Here

Click

Click

Click

① Choose **File**, **Back Up**.

② Insert a floppy disk. Or, click **Back Up to Hard Disk** and specify an alternative name or location for the backup file by editing the text box or using the **Browse** button.

③ Click the **OK** button.

End Task

Task 17: Opening Another Money File

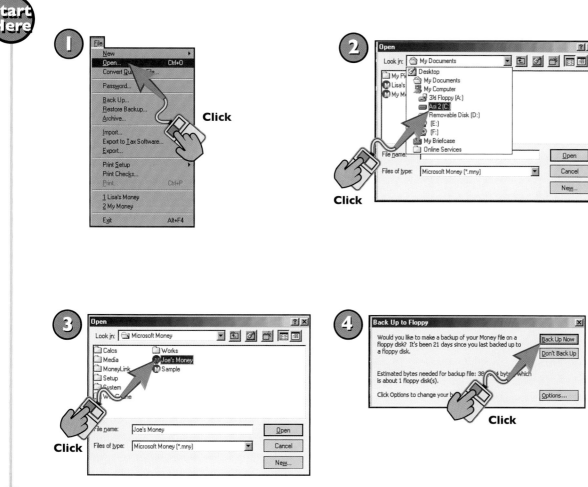

Click

Click

Click

Click

Choosing the Money File to Use

Task 2 explained how to create a new Money file to separate the financial data for each Money user. All subsequent tasks have assumed you were working in the correct Money file. When the time comes to switch users, you can open the needed Money file, as described in this task.

✓ **New Year, New File**
If your finances are simple and you don't use the budgeting or reports features in Money, you also can create a new Money file each year. When you need to refer to the prior year's file, you can open it.

✓ **Adding Password Protection**
You can add a password to any Money file to control which household members can open the file. Choose the **File, Password** command, enter the password in the **New Password** text box, and click **OK**.

---

1 Choose **File**, **Open**.

2 If needed, use the Look In drop-down list and file list to select the disk and folder that holds the file.

3 Double-click the file to open in the list of files in the Open dialog box.

4 Click **Back Up Now** to back up the previously opened Money file before it closes.

x

Going Internet with Internet Explorer 5 and Outlook Express 5

Web browser software enables you to look at information posted in special locations on the Internet. Web browsers display pages with attractive formatting that can include sounds, animated pictures, products you can purchase online, and more. With ***e-mail software***, you can trade online messages and files with friends and family, and in some cases participate in public forums called ***newsgroups***. Part 4 shows you how to use Internet Explorer 5.0 and Outlook Express 5.0, the updated browser and e-mail programs that Works Suite 2000 installs.

Tasks

Launching and Exiting Internet Explorer

The *World Wide Web* (the *Web*), a collection of computers on the Internet, stores and presents information graphically. To view Web information, you use *Web browser* software. Microsoft Works Suite 2000 includes the Internet Explorer 5.0 Web browser. When you launch Internet Explorer, it prompts you to use your computer modem to dial your Internet connection with an *Internet service provider* (ISP). When you close Internet Explorer, it reminds you to disconnect from the Internet.

✓ **Establishing Your Connection**
If you've just obtained an account with an ISP and need to set up your Internet connection, see Appendix A, "Setting Up Your Internet Connection."

Task 1: Launching and Exiting Internet Explorer

Start Here

1 Internet Explorer
Click

2 Dial-up Connection
Select the service you want to connect to, and then enter your user name and password.
Connect to: Lisa's Mindspring
User name: mm558866
Password: ********
☑ Save password
☐ Connect automatically
Connect   Settings...   Work Offline
Click

3 File
New
Open...   Ctrl+O
Edit with Microsoft Word for Windows
Save   Ctrl+S
Save As...
Page Setup...
Print...   Ctrl+P
Send
Import and Export...
Properties
Work Offline
Close
Click

4 Auto Disconnect
Do you want to close the connection to Lisa's Mindspring?
☐ Don't use Auto Disconnect
Stay Connected   Disconnect Now
Click

1 Double-click the **Internet Explorer** icon on the desktop.

2 Click **Connect** in the Dial-Up Connection dialog box to dial your Internet connection.

3 When you finish a session in Internet Explorer (see Tasks 2–8), choose **File**, **Close** to exit.

4 Click **Disconnect Now** to disconnect from the Internet.

End Task

Task 2: Using a URL to Jump to a Web Page

Start Here

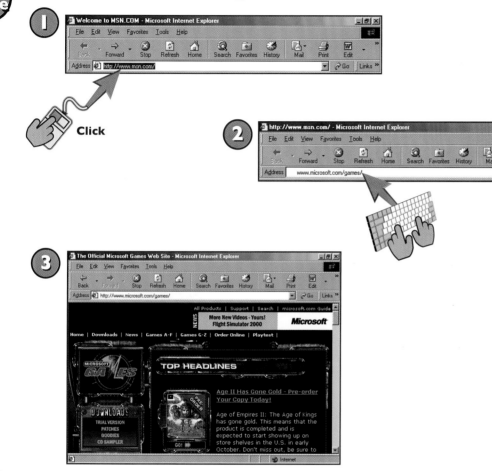

Click

End Task

Using a URL

The Web stores information in **Web pages.** The Web identifies each Web page with a **Web address** called the **Uniform Resource Locator (URL).** Each Web URL consists of the **content identifier,** http://, which identifies the address as a Web address. The rest of the address, its location, identifies the **Web site** (www.microsoft.com), directory (/games/), and a page name (default.htm), which is optional. So, a full Web address looks like http://www.microsoft.com /games/ or http:// reference.msn.com/defaul t.asp?pagename=parent. To display a particular Web page (called *browsing*), you can enter its address in Internet Explorer.

✓ **What's a Site?**
A **Web site** is a particular computer (or designated storage area on such a computer) that holds Web pages and is connected to the Internet.

1. Click the URL in the **Address** bar at the top of the Explorer Window (or drag over the URL) to highlight it.

2. Type the URL of the page to view and press **Enter**.

3. When the Web page appears, you can read it or browse to other pages.

Using a Link

Web pages offer *links* (or *hyperlinks*) to other Web pages. Click the link to jump to the page it represents (also called "following the link"). A link can be text highlighted with a special color or underlining, a button or graphic on the page, a tab or a pop-up menu selection, or something else. After you use a link to display a particular page and then return to the page holding that link, Explorer changes the link text's color or perhaps adds a border around a link button so that you can tell which links you've already followed.

✓ Finding Links

When you point to a link item, the pointer might change into a hand. The status bar at the bottom of the Explorer window displays the URL address or shortcut the link represents, and a pop-up description might appear.

Task 3: Clicking a Link to Display Another Page

Start Here

Click

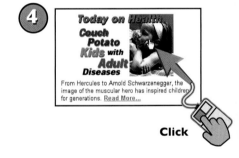

Click

(1) Point to a text link until you see the hand pointer and the status bar identifies the link.

(2) Click the text link to display the linked page.

(3) Point to a linked graphic until you see the hand pointer and the status bar identifies the link.

(4) Click the linked graphic to display the linked page.

End Task

Task 4: Backing Up or Going Forward

Start Here

End Task

Using Back and Forward

Internet Explorer's Back and Forward buttons work somewhat like the Rewind and Fast Forward controls for your VCR. You can click the Back button to return to a page you've previously viewed. Click Back multiple times to move back through several successive pages. After you've moved back, click the Forward button to redisplay successive pages in the order in which you originally displayed them.

✓ Jumping Around
If you want to jump directly to a particular page rather than backing up or moving forward through multiple pages, click the drop-down list arrow beside the Address drop-down list and click the URL for the page you want to display. Or, click the drop-down list arrow for the Back or Forward button and select the desired page.

1 To move back, point to the **Back** button to see a pop-up description of the previous page.

2 Click the **Back** button to redisplay the previous page.

3 To move forward, point to the **Forward** button to see a pop-up description of the next page.

4 Click the **Forward** button to redisplay the next page.

Adding a Favorite Page

You can mark a Web page you like or often use so you can quickly display it at any time. Basically, you create a shortcut, called a *favorite*, that you can select to jump to the page rather than entering the URL for the page. The favorite represents the Web page's URL. Explorer stores the favorites you mark on the Favorites menu or in the Favorites list that appears when you click the Favorites toolbar button.

⚠ WARNING

Don't bother adding a page with a short lifespan to your list of Favorites, such as an article from an online magazine. Instead, choose **File**, **Save As** to display the Save As dialog box. Use the Save In list to specify a disk and folder to save the file to, enter a name for the file in the **File Name** text box, and then click **Save**. This saves the article as an **HTML** file (a Web page file) on your hard disk.

Task 5: Adding a Page to Your List of Favorites

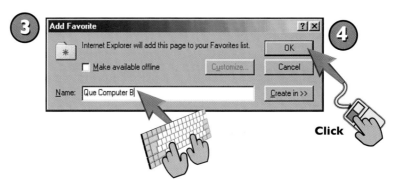

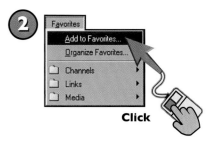

Click

Click

Display the Web page that you want to mark as a favorite page.

Choose **Favorites**, **Add to Favorites**.

If needed, edit the name for the favorite in the **Name** text box. This name appears on the Favorites menu or list.

Click **OK** to finish adding the favorite to your list.

Task 6: Displaying a Favorite Page

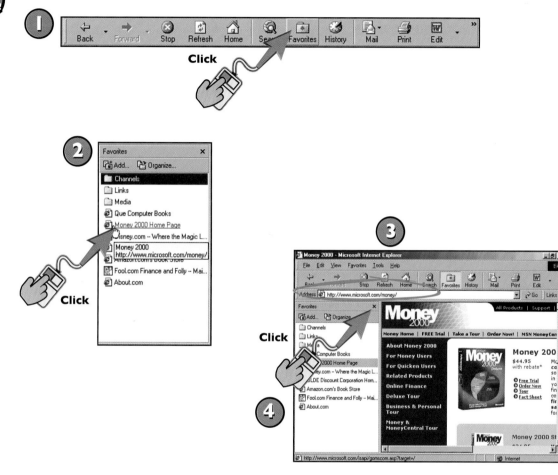

Click

Click

Click

Displaying a Favorite Page

After you've marked a favorite page as described in Task 5, the name you specified for the favorite appears on the Favorites menu and the list that appears when you click the Favorites button. To display a favorite page, select its name from the Favorites menu or Favorites list.

✓ **Handling an Obsolete Favorite**

If a favorite no longer works because the Web page has been deleted or its address has changed, you can delete the favorite. See Task 7 to see a tip about deleting a favorite.

✓ **Grouping Your Favorites**

You can store your favorites in specific folders to organize favorites by topic, such as Health, Finances, or Games. See Task 7 to learn how to create folders and move favorites into them.

① Click the **Favorites** button or **Favorites** menu.

② Click the name of the favorite page you want to display in the list or menu.

③ When the favorite page appears, you can review it, click links, or display another page.

④ Click the **Favorites** button again to close the list, if needed.

End Task

Organizing Your Favorites

If you add numerous favorites to your list, the list can become lengthy and unwieldy. Scanning through a list of 40 favorites could take as much time as entering a URL. To ensure that your favorites continue to save you time, you can create folders to group the favorites by topic, such as Health, Finances, Cars, Crafts, and so on. Placing your favorites into folders gives you more control over how Explorer lists the favorites. The Favorites list displays each folder name; select the folder to display the favorites you've placed in that folder, which appear in a submenu.

Tweaking Your Favorites List

By default, Explorer lists your favorites in alphabetical order. You can edit the name of a favorite to ensure it's listed as you prefer.

Task 7: Organizing Your Favorites

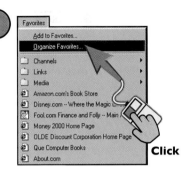

Click

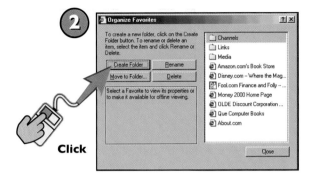

Click

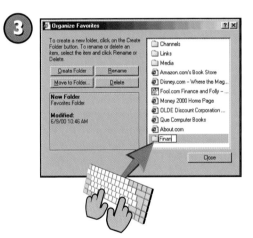

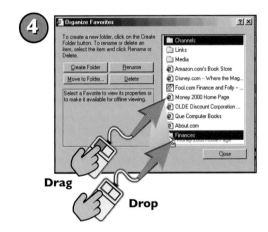

Drag

Drop

Choose **Favorites**, **Organize Favorites**.

Click the **Create Folder** button.

Type a new folder name, which appears beside the folder icon, and press **Enter**.

Drag a favorite and drop it onto the folder icon to move the favorite into that folder.

Next Step

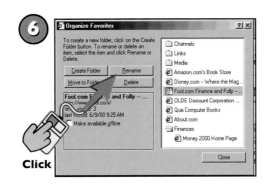

Deleting a Favorite

You can delete an old favorite by using the **Organize Favorites dialog box. Click the name of the Favorite to delete, and then click the Delete button.**

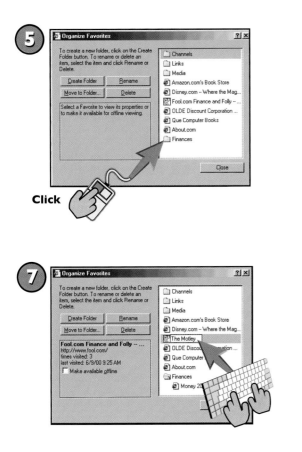

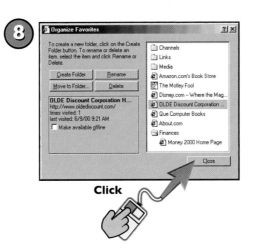

Double-click a folder's icon to view the favorites it holds.

To rename a selected folder or favorite, click the Rename button.

Type the new name and press **Enter**.

Click the **Close** button to finish organizing favorites.

Finding Favorites in Folders

To use a favorite that you've stored in a folder, point to the folder in the Favorites menu, and click the favorite name. In the Favorites list, double-click the folder icon and click the favorite name.

End Task

Task 8: Searching for Information

Using a Search

Internet Explorer offers a built-in way to use your choice of several search services offered on the Web, such as Yahoo!, Excite, Lycos, and Infoseek, as well as the **MSN Web Search**. You enter the *search words* (topic) you want to find, and the search service searches its catalog of registered pages and lists the matching pages. Click a listed page to display it in Explorer and click the **Print** button to print it.

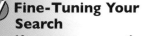 **Fine-Tuning Your Search**

If you enter more than one search word, as in *organic gardening*, most search tools list Web pages that contain any of the search words. To display only pages that contain all the search words you enter, type quotation marks around the search words or use a plus sign or **AND** between them.

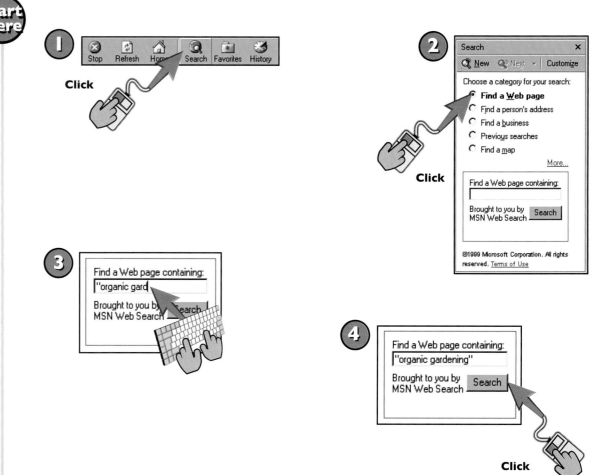

Click

Click

Click

 Click the **Search** button. (It doesn't matter what Web page is currently displayed.)

Click to choose a search category, if search categories appear.

Type your search word(s) in the search text box.

Click the **Search** button. (This button might have another name for some search tools.)

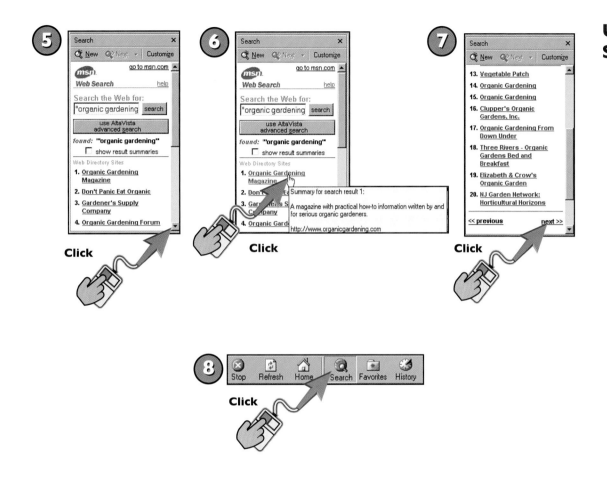

Using Your Favorite Search Tool

Microsoft has set up Explorer and its Web site to randomly use a different search tool in the Search pane each time you click the **Search** button. To use only your favorite search tool, click the **Customize** button in the Search pane. Click the **Use One Search Service for All Searches** option button, click the service you want in the **Choose the Search Service** list, and click **OK**.

(5) Click the **down** scroll arrow to scroll through the search results list, which offers links to matching sites and pages.

(6) Click a link to display a page that contains the search words you entered.

(7) Click the **Next** and **Previous** links at the bottom of the search frame to find and use additional search results listings.

(8) Click the **Search** button again to conclude the search.

✓ Organizing Search Results

Some search tools organize the search results list by category. Others offer you ways to refine your search or find other pages similar to one listed in the search results.

Task 9: Downloading a File

Downloading a File

To attract you to a Web site, its publisher might offer files you can download, such as research documents, software, sound files, software patches, or graphics. If you encounter a link to a file download, it's easy to use that link to download the file and save it to your hard disk. The Internet (and Internet Explorer) uses a communication method called *FTP* (*file transfer protocol*) to transfer files to your system from a Web site.

✓ Sharing the Software Load

Most software downloaded from the Web is *shareware*. You can download the shareware to test it out, but you should send a modest payment to the shareware author. Shareware works on the honor system, so please do your part and pay your shareware fees.

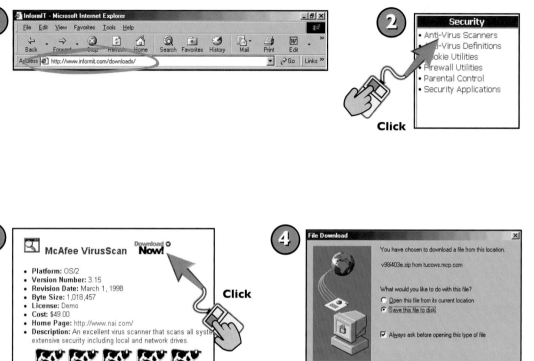

(1) Display the Web page that offers categories of downloadable files.

(2) Click links, if needed, to navigate to the category that holds the file to download.

(3) Click the link or button for the file to download.

(4) Leave Save This File to Disk selected in the dialog box that appears and click **OK**.

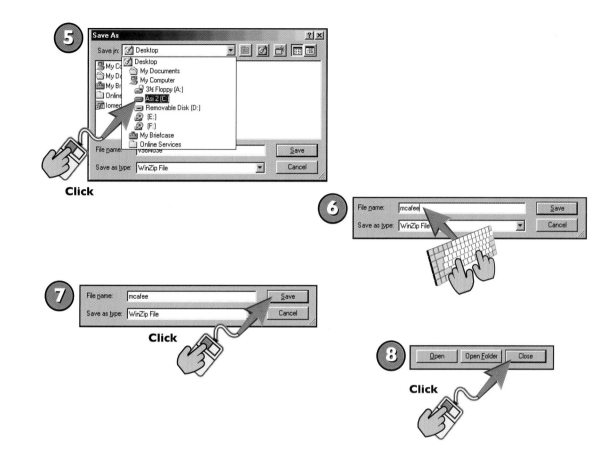

Looking Out for Viruses

Any file you download from the Web (Internet) could be infected with a computer *virus*, a program designed to alter how your computer works or even damage information on your system. If you plan to download files often, you should purchase and install an antivirus program such as **McAfee VirusScan**, **Thunderbyte Antivirus**, or **Norton Antivirus**.

✔ **Grabbing a Graphic File**

If you like a graphic you see on a Web page, you usually can save it to your hard disk to use it for personal purposes. To try to save a graphic or picture, right-click it and click **Save Picture As**. Use the Save in list to choose the disk to save to, and click **Save**. Or right-click the picture and click **Set As Wallpaper** to use it on your Windows desktop.

⑤ Choose a disk (and folder) to save the file to from the **Save In** list.

⑥ Edit the filename, if needed.

⑦ Click **Save**.

⑧ After the file downloads, click **Close** to close the Download Complete dialog box.

End Task

Displaying Online Tasks from the Task Launcher

Works Suite offers a number of tasks that take you to the MSN Web site from Microsoft to perform various operations like finding a home that's for sale. If you prefer to work from the Task Launcher instead of surfing on your own in Internet Explorer, you can follow the steps here.

Task 10: Displaying Online Works Suite Tasks

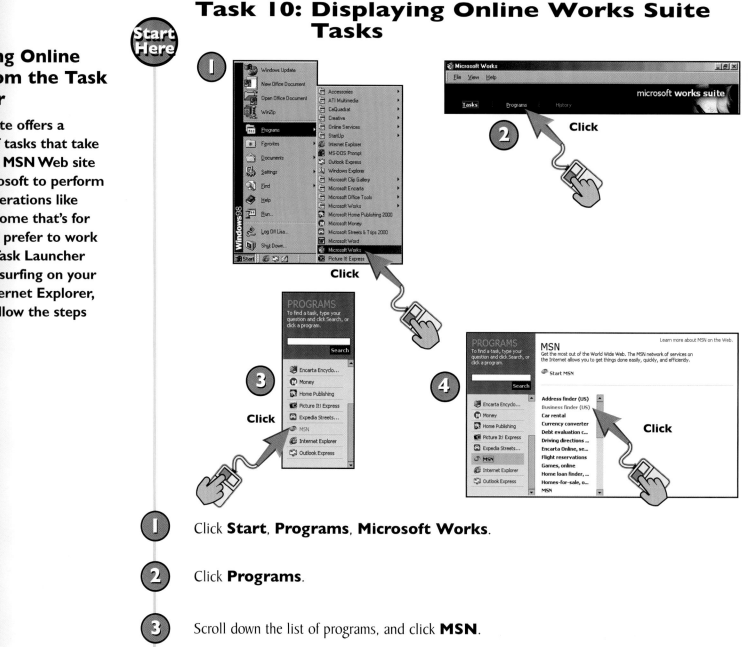

Start Here

Click

Click

Click

Click

Click Start, Programs, Microsoft Works.

Click Programs.

Scroll down the list of programs, and click MSN.

Click the desired task in the list of tasks.

Next Step

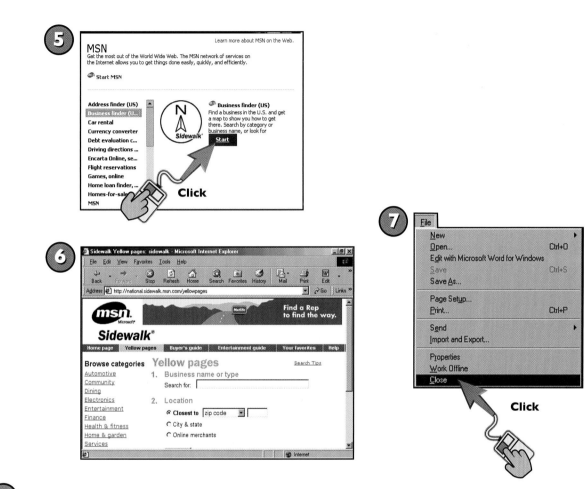

Learning More About Works

If you want more information about Works, choose **Help, Microsoft On the Web, Microsoft Works Home Page** from the Task Launcher.

⑤ Click the **Start** button and connect to the Internet, if prompted.

⑥ Browse or use the Web page that appears.

⑦ Choose **File**, **Close** to finish and disconnect from the Internet when prompted.

⚠ WARNING
If you can't find the Auto Disconnect dialog box to close your Internet connection, try closing the Works Suite Window or use the Windows taskbar.

Task 11: Creating an Address Book Entry

Tracking Your Contacts

Over time, you can correspond with dozens of friends and family members via Outlook Express. (The next task explains how to send e-mail messages.) Although you could type each e-mail address in by hand, good luck remembering them all. Instead, Outlook provides its own *Address Book* program that you can use to keep track of names and e-mail addresses.

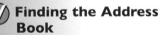 **Finding the Address Book**

You also can start the Address Book by choosing **Start, Programs, Microsoft Works, Address Book** from the Windows taskbar or by clicking the **Addresses** button on the Outlook Express toolbar.

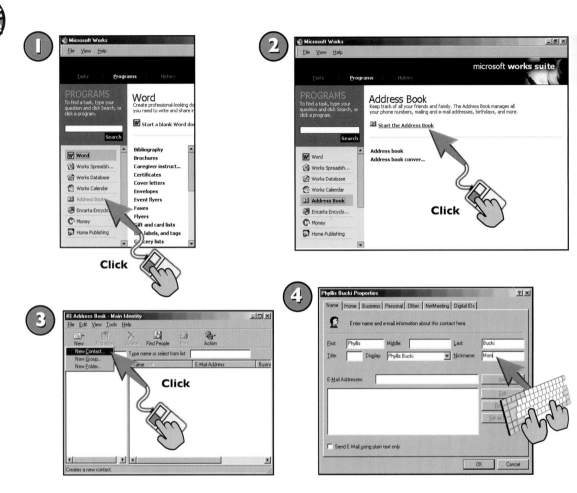

Click **Programs** in the Works Suite Task Launcher, and click Address Book.

Click **Start the Address Book**.

Click the **New** button, and click **New Contact**.

Enter basic contact information on the Name tab of the Properties window.

 Next Step

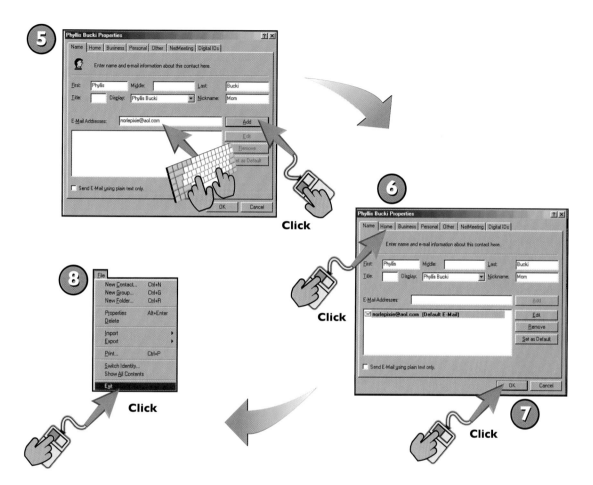

Editing Contact Information

If information about a contact changes, you can edit contact information in the Address Book. Click the contact's name in the list of contacts in the Address Book window, and click the Properties button. Make changes on the tabs in the Properties window as needed. Click OK to finish the changes.

Click

Click

Click

Click

(5) Enter the person's e-mail address in the **E-Mail Addresses** text box, and click **Add**.

(6) Click any other tabs in the dialog box as needed, and enter additional contact information.

(7) Click **OK** to finish entering the contact information.

(8) After repeating steps 3–7 to enter additional addresses, choose **File**, **Exit** in the Address Book window to close the Address Book.

✔ **Identifying Yourself**
If multiple family members use Outlook Express and have different contacts, you can create a separate Address Book identity for each family member to keep those contacts separate. Use the File, Switch Identity command in Address Book to create and select identities.

Mailing Without Stamps

As families scatter over the country and world via hot job opportunities, e-mail helps everyone stay in touch. Sending e-mail messages can be faster than regular mail, and less expensive than lengthy long distance calls. You can even attach files with your messages, such as scanned pictures of the kids or party planning information. You use Outlook Express to send your e-mail via Works Suite or Windows.

✅ **Starting, Starting, Starting**

You also can start Outlook Express by clicking the **Launch Outlook Express** button on the Quick Launch toolbar; by double-clicking the **Outlook Express** shortcut on the Windows desktop; or by choosing **Start, Programs, Outlook Express.**

Task 12: Starting Outlook and Sending an E-Mail Message

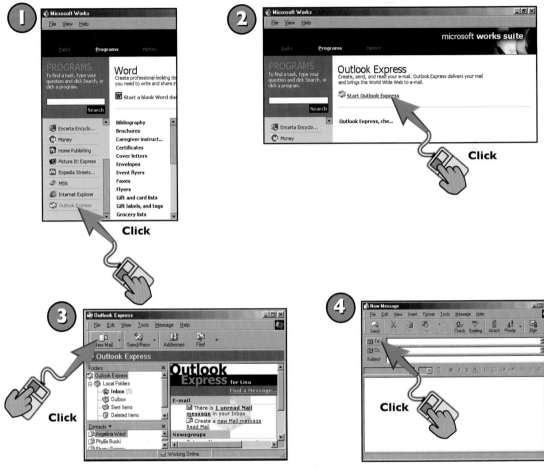

Click

Click

Click

Click

Click

① Click **Programs** in the Works Suite Task Launcher, and then click **Outlook Express** at the bottom of the list.

② Click **Start Outlook Express**. Connect to the Internet if prompted.

③ Click the **New Mail** button.

④ Click the **To:** button.

Next Step

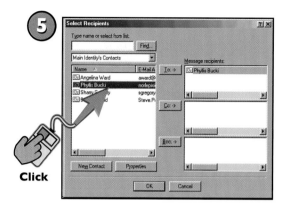

Click

Attaching a File to Your Message

To include a file attachment with a message, click the **Attach** button in the message window. Use the **Look In** list in the Insert Attachment dialog box to navigate to the folder that holds the file you want. Click the file to attach, and click **Attach**.

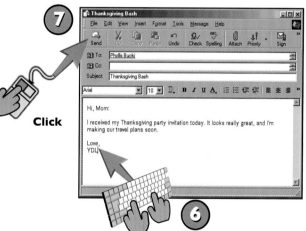

Click

☑ **Typing It**
You can type an e-mail address directly into the **To:** or **Cc:** text boxes in the New Message window.

☑ **Offline to Online**
If you chose not to connect to the Internet before composing your message and click **Send**, Outlook displays a Send Mail message. Click **OK**. Later, click the **Send/Recv** button in Outlook Express. You'll be prompted to connect to the Internet. Do so to send the message.

5 Double-click each contact to whom you'd like to address the message, and then click **OK**.

6 Enter the subject and body of your message.

7 Click **Send** to send the message. Outlook sends the message immediately if your system is connected to the Internet.

Task 13: Retrieving and Reading E-Mail

Reading Incoming Messages

When another user sends you messages, you need to check your e-mail in Outlook Express to find those messages. Outlook connects to the Internet if needed and transfers messages for you from your ISP's mail server to your Outlook Express Inbox. From there, you can read and manage your messages as needed.

Start Here

Click

Click

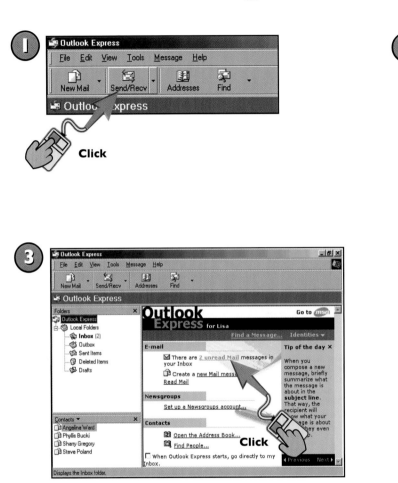

Click

✓ **To the Max**
The Outlook Express window might not be maximized when it first appears. Click the window Maximize button in the upper-right corner to enlarge the window.

Click the **Send/Recv** button in Outlook Express.

Click **Connect** to connect to the Internet if prompted. (Click **Yes** first if you also see a message window.)

After messages download, click the link to your new messages.

Next Step

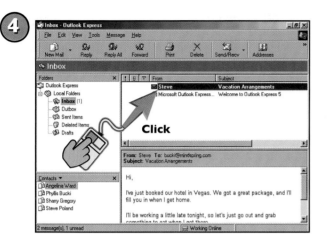

Click

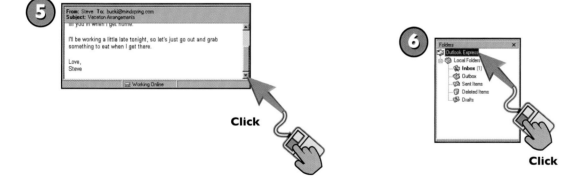

Click

Filing Your E-Mail

You can add your own custom folders in Outlook Express to divide received messages. This approach reduces Inbox clutter and helps you find older messages. To create a new folder, just right-click the **Local Folders** choice in the Folders list, and then click **New Folder**. Enter a name in the **Folder Name** text box, and click **OK**. To move a message into the new folder, click the **Inbox** icon. Drag the message from the list at the right and drop it onto the icon for the new folder. Double-click the icon for the new folder to see the messages it holds.

Click

4️⃣ In the right pane of the Inbox, click the message you want to read.

5️⃣ Scroll to read more of your message, if needed.

6️⃣ Click Outlook Express (in the left pane) to return to the initial Outlook screen.

✅ **Seeing More**
If you double-click a new e-mail message in the Inbox list, the message opens in its own, larger window. This makes the message easier to read.

Task 14: Setting Up a News Server

Adding a News Account

Online *newsgroups* hold publicly posted messages. Each newsgroup holds messages relating to a particular topic, such as a particular band or piece of software. *News (NNTP) servers* on the Internet hold the newsgroups and their messages. Your ISP should provide you with information about the news server it hosts for its customers. To access that news server or any other public news server, you need to set up an account for it in Outlook Express.

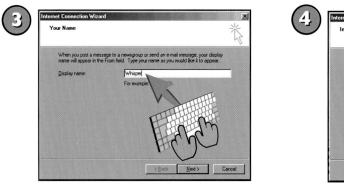

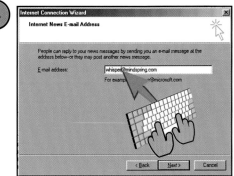

✓ **Name Game**
News server names typically look like
news.mindspring.com.

① Choose **Tools**, **Accounts** in Outlook Express.

② Click the **Add** button, and click **News**.

③ If needed, edit the entry in the **Display Name** text box. Click **Next**.

④ If needed, edit the **E-Mail Address** text box entry.

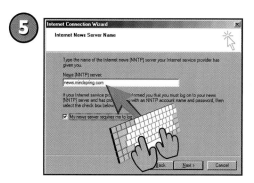

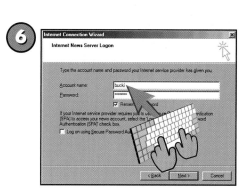

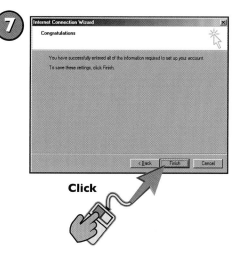

Click

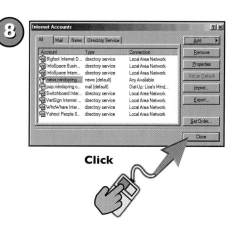

Click

Using Your "Alias"

If you use your real name and e-mail address in newsgroups, you might have solicitation e-mails arriving on a daily or hourly basis. To make a nickname for yourself instead of your real name, make a nickname entry in step 3, and adjust your e-mail address by adding extra characters in step 4. Then, you can include instructions with your newsgroup posts as to how to send you real e-mail by deleting the extra characters. This technique prevents solicitors from using automated methods to gather your e-mail address from your posts.

---

5 Enter the **News (NNTP) Server** address and check the **My News Server Requires Me to Log On** check box. Click **Next**.

6 Enter your **Account Name** and **Password**. Click **Next**.

7 Click **Finish**.

8 Click **Close**. You can connect and download newsgroups now, or do so later as described in the next task.

✔ **Account Name**
Your account name is the first part of your e-mail address—typically, not your overall Internet account user ID. The password is the same as for your Internet account logon or e-mail account.

Task 15: Refreshing the Newsgroup List

Listing Newsgroups

News servers hold thousands of newsgroups, and the list changes over time. If you've just added the news account to Outlook Express, you need to download the newsgroup list to your system, and choose which newsgroups to use. From time to time, you should repeat this process to refresh the list, so you can view and subscribe to new newsgroups.

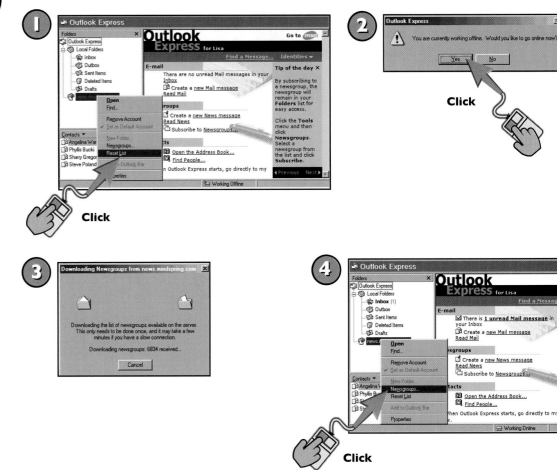

Start Here

Click

Click

Click

(1) Right-click the name of the news server in the Folders list, and click **Reset List**.

(2) If you're prompted to go online, click **Yes**, and then **Connect**.

(3) If you need to interrupt the newsgroup download, click **Cancel**. Otherwise, it will take a few minutes.

(4) When the download concludes, right-click the news server and click **Newsgroups**.

Next Step

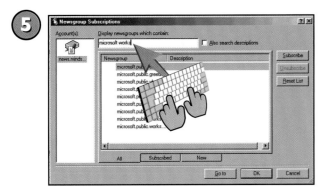

Choosing Newsgroups to Read

When you subscribe to a newsgroup, you tell Outlook that you want it to retrieve the posts (messages) from that group so that you can read them.

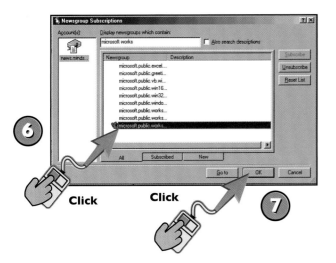

Click   Click

⑤ Scroll through the list, or enter a term to display matching newsgroups. (Delete the term to redisplay the full list.)

⑥ Double-click each newsgroup you want to subscribe to.

⑦ After repeating steps 6 and 7 to select all your newsgroups, click **OK**.

⑧ Review your newsgroups in the Folders list.

✅ **Cancel My Subscription**
When you no longer want to subscribe to a newsgroup, double-click it on the Subscribed tab of the Newsgroup Subscriptions window.

Task 16: Reading Newsgroup Messages

Updating the Message List

When you're ready to read your news, you need to synchronize the newsgroups you've selected to display the current list of messages. You need to synchronize newsgroups each time you want to read messages or posts to ensure that you have the most recent list of messages. New messages come on as soon as users post them, and old messages scroll off after a designated period of time.

✓ In Sync

To change the synchronization settings for a newsgroup, click it in the list, click the **Settings** button, and click a new synchronization choice. For example, you might want to download only the message headers, because downloading the messages, too, can take quite some time.

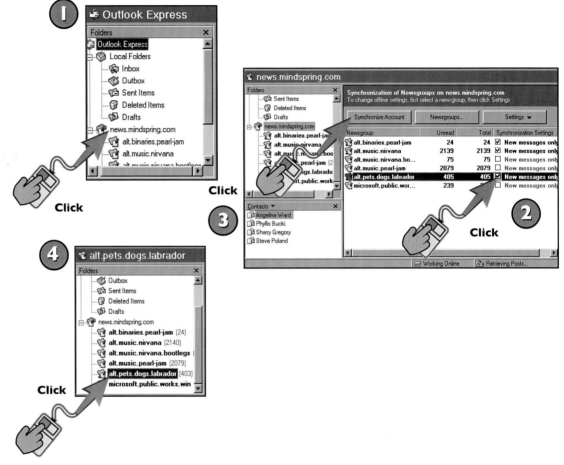

1. Click the name of the news server in the Folders list.

2. Check each newsgroup to synchronize.

3. Click **Synchronize Account**.

4. When the message download concludes, click the newsgroup to read in the Folders list.

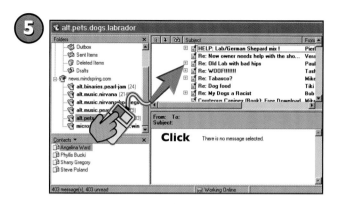

⑤

Reading a Particular Message

Each newsgroup you follow might have hundreds of messages posted at any given time. You can scroll through the postings to find ones of interest, and then display each one you'd like to read.

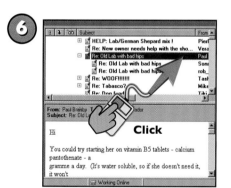

⑥

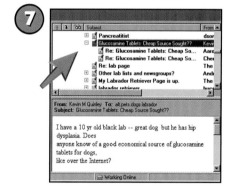

⑦

⑤ Scroll through the list of messages, and click the plus beside any message to display all the messages in the thread.

⑥ Click on each message in the thread to read its text in the pane below.

⑦ Repeat steps 4 through 6 to read other messages.

✔ **Keeping the Thread**
An original post and all the responses to it are collectively known as a thread.

Task 17: Posting to a Newsgroup and Exiting Outlook

Going Public with Your Thoughts

Newsgroups exist to foster public participation. If you're looking for advice about an issue or would like to offer your opinion about someone's question, you can send in your posting or response to the newsgroup.

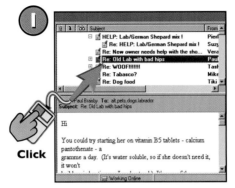

Click

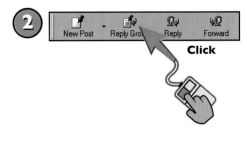

Click

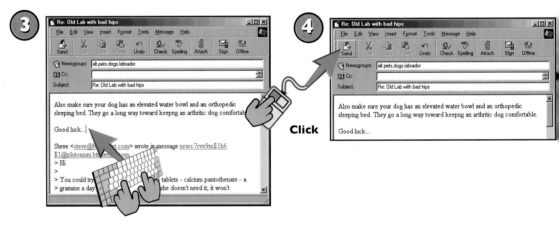

Click

1. If you want to respond to a particular message, click it in the list.

2. Click **Reply Group** to respond to the message. (To create a new thread, skip step 1 and click **New Post** here instead.)

3. Enter your message response.

4. Click the **Send** button in the message window.

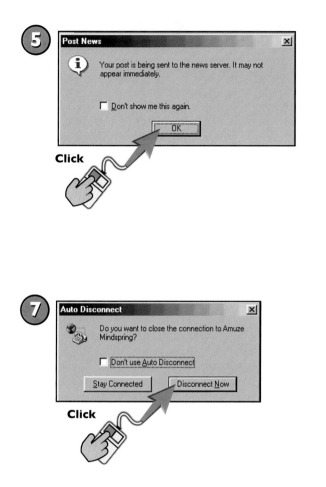

Click

Click

Click

Signing Off

When you've finished working with mail and newsgroups, you should close **Outlook Express** and disconnect from the Internet, if needed. Depending on your connection plan, you can save significant money by not inadvertently staying online.

⑤ Click **OK** to the message that tells you your post will appear online soon.

⑥ Choose **File**, **Exit**.

⑦ Click **Disconnect Now**.

✓ Works Away
Also close the Works Suite Task Launcher if it happens to be open and you no longer need it.

5

Home Publishing and Picture It! Express

Part of the beauty of having a computer at home is that you can use it for any purpose that your time and software allow. Works Suite offers two applications that enable you to use your computer to explore and create. This part shows you how to use Home Publishing to create projects such as cards, party decorations, and more.

Tasks

Launching Home Publishing with the Start Menu

How many times have you or your children spent hours with paper and markers to make cards, posters, or party banners? In many cases, such projects provide a great family activity. In other cases, you might want a faster method or more polished results. You can create a number of colorful projects in Microsoft's Home Publishing program. This task explains how to start the program and begin working.

✓ Other Starts

You also can use the **Start** menu to launch Home Publishing. Click **Start**, point to **Programs**, and then click **Microsoft Home Publishing 2000**. Or, if you're at the **Works Task Launcher**, click **Home Publishing** in the Programs list, and then click **Start Microsoft Home Publishing 2000**.

Task 1: Starting Home Publishing and Choosing a Project

Click

Click

Click

Click

 Insert the Works Suite Disc 5 CD into the CD-ROM drive, and click the **Start** button in the window that opens.

2 Click a tab at the left to choose a category of projects.

3 Click the button for the type of project to create.

4 Click to choose the specific type of card to create.

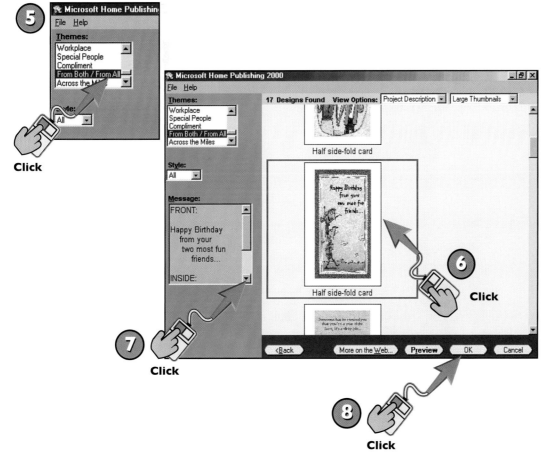

Designing a New Project

Most applications open a blank file for you. Because the types of projects you can create in Greetings Workshop vary dramatically, you must tell the program right off the bat what kind of project (file) you want to create. Follow the steps described here; then continue with the next few tasks to specify the project's contents and adjust how it looks.

⚠ WARNING
The tasks in this book depict creating a greeting card. The specific steps for different types of projects might vary. However, the techniques you learn for working with text and pictures apply in any project you create.

✔ Creating Subsequent Projects
After you create and save your first project, choose **File, Close and Return to Opening Screen** to start a new project.

5 Click a choice in the **Themes** list.

6 Scroll down through the designs and click on the one you want.

7 Scroll down the message text box to review the message for the selected card.

8 Click **OK** to finish creating the project.

Task 2: Adding and Editing Text

Entering Project Content

Unless your card's interior message (or the text in another type of project) happens to match the name and text you need, you must edit it and add new text, if applicable. Home Publishing presents the opportunity to do so immediately after you create the project and choose its mood and design.

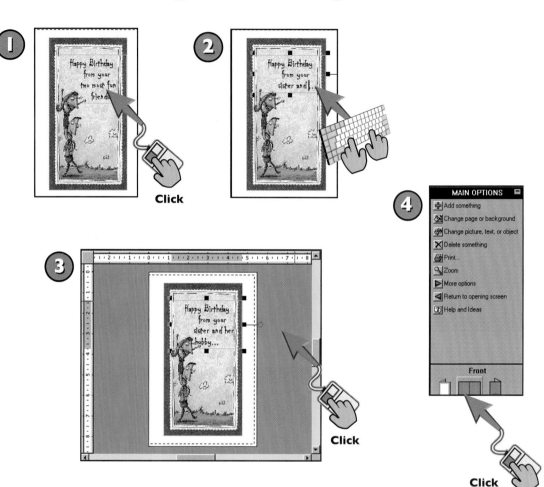

Start Here

Click

Click

Click

MAIN OPTIONS
- Add something
- Change page or background
- Change picture, text, or object
- Delete something
- Print...
- Zoom
- More options
- Return to opening screen
- Help and Ideas

Front

① Click on the text box holding the text to edit.

② Click to position the insertion point within the text, and then edit it as needed.

③ Click in a gray area outside the project or in the blank margin to finish the edit and deselect the text box.

④ View another page or area in the Project.

Next Step

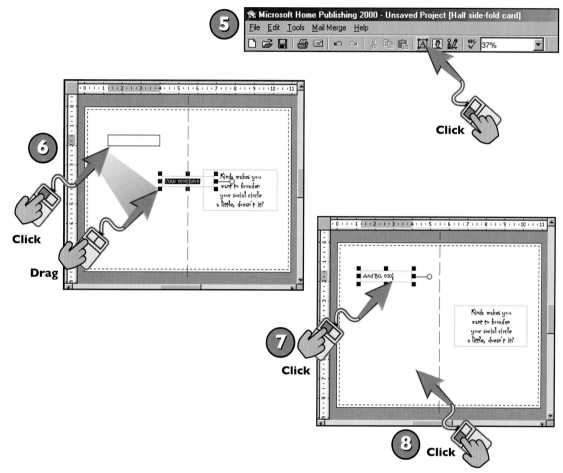

Viewing Project Information

After you select the look and text for your card or other project, you can work with particular elements such as blocks of text or graphics. You can zoom in to get a closer look at what you're working with, and then zoom back out to see the results. In addition, you can display a particular page. To zoom in or out, click on **Zoom** in the Main Options list, and then click a zoom choice. Use the buttons in the lower-left corner of the Home Publishing screen to view a different page in the project.

Click

Click

Click

Click

Drag

Click

5 — Click the **Add New Text** button on the toolbar.

6 — Drag the new text box to the desired location.

7 — Type your new text to replace the placeholder text. The text box expands in size to accommodate the text you enter.

8 — Click outside the text to finish entering.

✓ **Different Projects, Different Views**
The available pages to view depend on the type of project you created. For example, several different projects don't have multiple pages.

End Task

Task 3: Changing the Look of Page Text

Formatting Text

Each text box in the project you create uses text formatting meant to complement the design you selected for the project. That doesn't prevent you from doing your own thing, though. For example, if you enter very little text in a text box, you might want to make the text larger. You can apply another font and size to the text: Make it bold, italic, or underlined; change it to outline-style; add a drop-shadow; change the alignment within the box; or change the color.

✅ **Pressing the Buttons**
When you click a button to apply formatting to text, the button takes on a depressed appearance. To remove the formatting, click the button again.

✅ **Expanding Text Boxes**
When you make text larger, the text box holding it automatically expands in size.

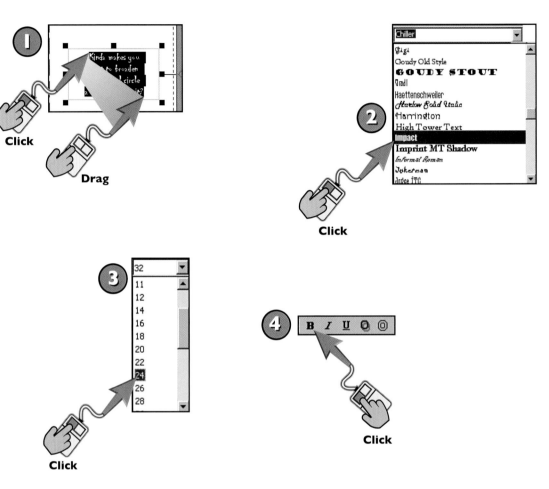

① Drag over the text to select it.

② Open the **Font** drop-down list, scroll it, and click a new font for the text.

③ Open the **Font Size** drop-down list and click the font size to use.

④ To toggle **Bold**, **Italic**, **Underline**, **Shadow**, or **Outline** on or off, click the button for that effect.

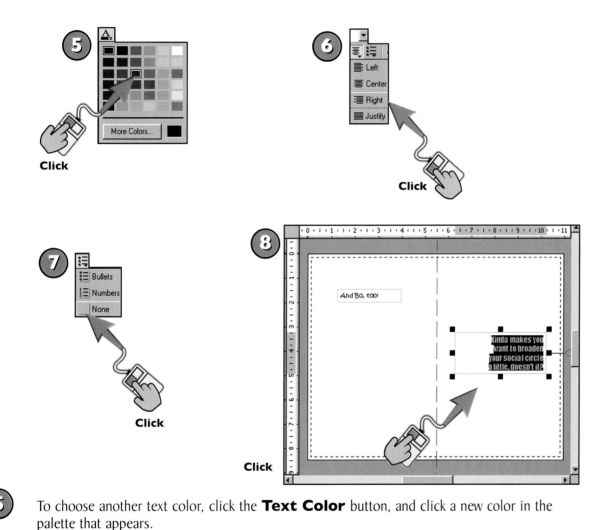

Click

Click

Click

Click

And Bo, too!

Kinda makes you want to broaden your social circle a little, doesn't it?

Removing an Object from a Project

If you've drawn objects, created a text box, or worked with clip art in a Word document, you can click on an object and press the **Delete** key to remove it from a document. In a Home Publishing project, it takes a bit more to delete a text box, a picture you've inserted, or another element. Click the **Delete Something** choice in the Main Options screen to start. Click the first option, **Picture, Text, or Other Object**, and then click the Object to delete. You also can click a choice on the Delete Something menu to delete the page border or background.

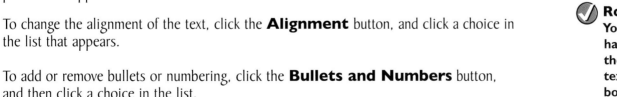

5 To choose another text color, click the **Text Color** button, and click a new color in the palette that appears.

6 To change the alignment of the text, click the **Alignment** button, and click a choice in the list that appears.

7 To add or remove bullets or numbering, click the **Bullets and Numbers** button, and then click a choice in the list.

8 Click outside the text box to finish your changes.

✔ **Rotation Situation**
You can drag the rotation handle that extends from the right side of selected text box to rotate the text box.

End Task

Task 4: Adding a Picture or Photo

Inserting a Greetings Workshop Picture

Home Publishing calls its predrawn clip art images and graphic images from other sources *pictures*. Most project designs include one or two pictures, but not necessarily on each page. You can add a picture to any page to make it even more colorful and interesting.

⚠ WARNING

To start the Clip Gallery, you must first insert Disc 4 of the Works Suite CD-ROM set in your CD-ROM drive. The Works Suite setup performs a minimum installation of Home Publishing, so you might see a prompt asking if you want to learn about reinstalling to reduce CD swapping. (Depending on the clip you select, you might even be prompted to insert another CD later.)

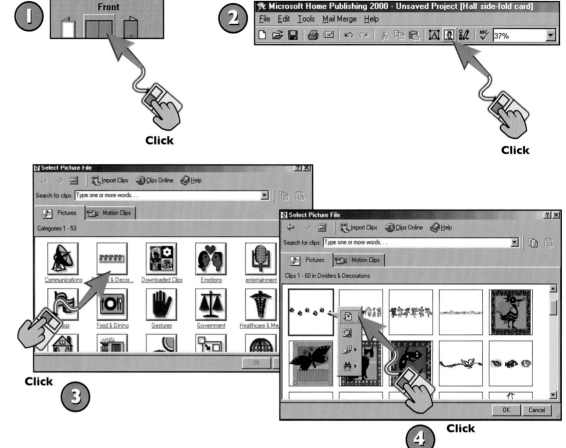

Click

① Display the page where you want to insert a picture.

② Click the **Add New Picture** button.

③ Scroll down, and click a picture category.

④ Scroll down, click the picture to insert, and click on the Insert Clip button.

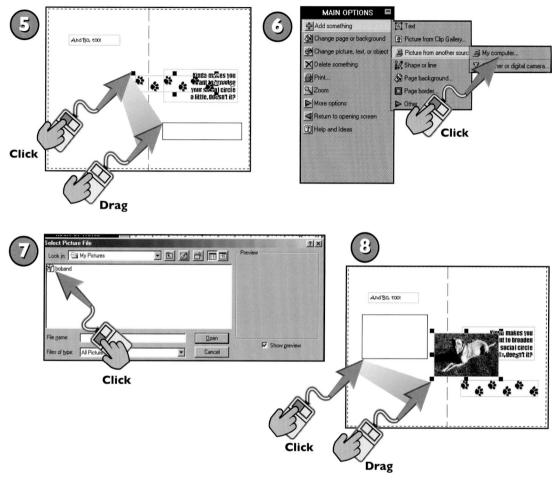

Inserting Your Own Photos

To personalize your projects in Home Publishing, insert a photo of your child or pet that you've snapped with your digital camera, scanned, or have had scanned. You can insert graphics you've drawn in a program such as Picture It! Express, too. You can insert any "photo" in the .bmp, .pcx, .gif, .jpg, .tif, or a number of other graphics formats into a project.

✅ **Pictures On-the-Fly**
Choose the **Scanner or Digital Camera** choice on the **Picture from Another Source** submenu if you have a scanner or digital camera hooked to your system and want to add an image directly from the device.

✅ **Deleting Pictures and Photos**
To delete a picture or photo from a page, click it to display selection handles. Click **Delete** in the **Picture Options** list at the left.

---

5 Drag the picture into place, drag one of its hands to resize it, and then click outside it.

6 Click **Add Something** in the Main Options list, and choose **Picture from Another Source**, **My Computer**.

7 Use the **Look In** list to navigate to the disk and folder holding your picture, and double-click on the picture file.

8 Drag the picture into place, drag one of its hands to resize it, and then click outside it.

Saving Your Work

Saving a project in Home Publishing resembles saving a project in other applications. When you save, you name the project file and specify where to store it on disk so that you can later open, edit, and print it as needed.

Task 5: Saving a Project

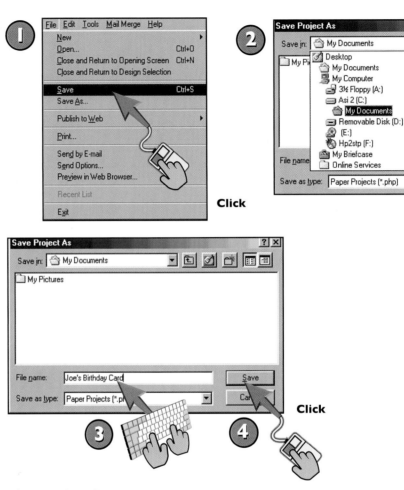

Click

Click

Click

Click

✓ **Saving Changes to a Project**

After you save and name your project file, click the **Save File** button to save your recent changes. You should resave the project every 10 minutes or so.

1 Choose **File**, **Save**.

2 If needed, use the **Save In** list to choose another disk and folder in which to save the file.

3 Edit the **File Name** text box entry as needed.

4 Click the **Save** button.

End Task

Task 6: Opening an Existing Project

Start Here

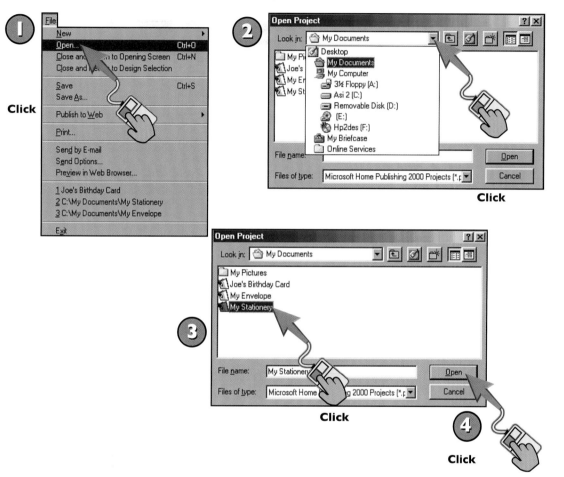

Click

Reopening a Project

Any time you're using Home Publishing, you can stop what you're doing and open a project you worked with earlier. After you open the project, you can make changes to it, save it, and print it.

✓ **Opening from the Opening Screen**
If you just started Home Publishing and you're at the opening screen, you can click the **My Projects** choice to open an existing project file stored in the C:\My Documents\ folder.

⚠ **WARNING**
Home Publishing enables you to have only one project open at a time. If you have a new project onscreen, be sure to save it before opening an existing file. If you don't, Home Publishing discards the new project without displaying any warning.

1 Choose **File**, **Open**.

2 If needed, use the **Look In** list to choose the disk and folder in which you saved the file.

3 Click the name of the project to open.

4 Click the **Open** button.

End Task

Task 7: Printing and Exiting

Finishing Your Work

Printing your project enables you to give copies to other people, or in the case of posters and banners, display it with pride. After you print your project, if you've finished working, you can exit Home Publishing.

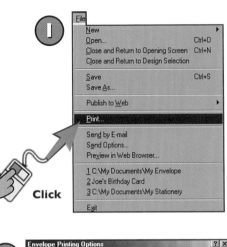

Start Here

Click

Click

Click

Click

Other Options

The type of project determines whether printing options are available in the Print dialog box. For example, for envelope projects, you can choose envelope feeding options. For banner projects, you can choose to print only a portion of the banner.

1 Choose **File**, **Print**.

2 Select the printer to use from the Name drop-down list.

3 If a button for printing options appears in the lower-left corner of the dialog box, click it.

4 Specify the options you want, and click **OK**.

Next Step

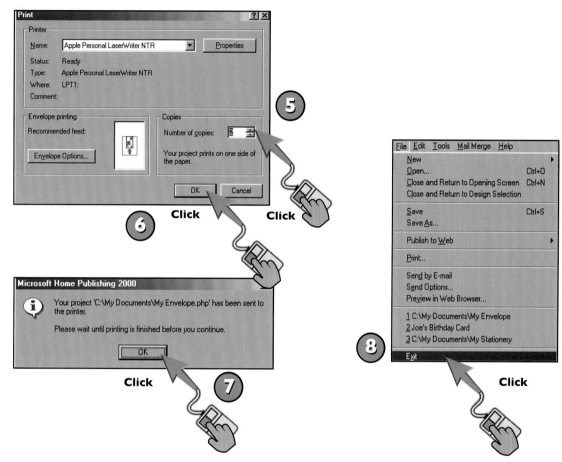

E-Mailing a Project

Rather than printing a project, you can e-mail it to other users, who can then view the project using Web browser software. To start the process for sending a project, choose **File, Send by E-Mail. Click As an Attachment in an E-Mail Message** in the list in the Send by E-Mail dialog box, and click **OK.** Home Publishing displays a message telling you it created a file named **RunMe.Exe** and placed the file in the **C:\My Documents\WebSend** folder. Click **Close.** Use Outlook Express to send the file as a file attachment. (See Task 12 in Part 4 to learn how.) The message recipient can then save and run the .exe file to view the Web-based greeting.

5 Click the **Number of Copies** to print up spinner button to increase the number of copies to print.

6 Click **OK**.

7 Inspect your printout and click **OK**.

8 Choose **File, Exit**. Click **Yes**, if needed, to save the project. If the Save Project As dialog box appears, enter a **File Name**, and then click **Save**.

Using Picture It! Express

After you start Picture It! Express, you have to choose a picture (graphic file) to start working with it. You can create a blank picture, open an existing picture from your hard disk, download a picture from a digital camera, or scan a new image directly into Picture It! Express. Although the steps for each operation are similar, there's only room here to show you two examples—scanning in an image and opening one from your hard disk.

 More Info Than Needed

On startup, you might see a few different windows asking you whether you want to change screen settings or view helpful videos. Click to check **Don't Show Me This Again** before clicking **OK**, **Close**, or **Yes** to eliminate these messages.

Task 8: Starting Picture It! and Getting a Picture

Start Here

Choose **Start**, **Programs**, **Picture It! Express**.

With your scanner on and a picture in the scanner, click **Scan Picture**. (Click another button here to download, open, or create a new picture.)

Verify the scan settings in the Scan Pictures area on the left side of the screen, and click **Scan**.

Click **Get Picture** in the menu on the left side of the Workbench tab, and click **Open Pictures**.

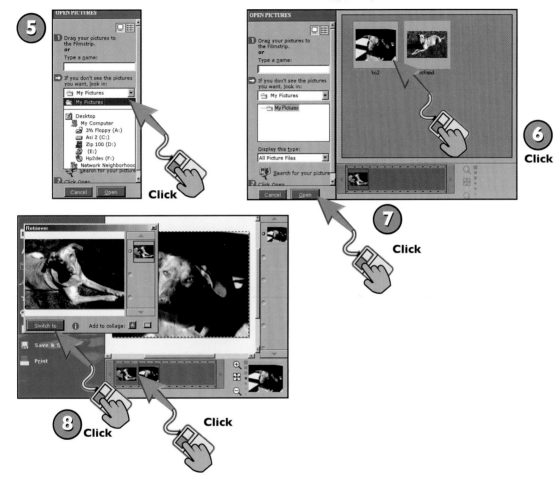

Adding Pictures to the Filmstrip

After you start Picture It! Express and open or create a new picture, the picture not only appears in the blank area at the left side of the Workbench tab, but also is loaded into the Filmstrip at the bottom of the screen. You can then open or create more pictures, which adds them to the Filmstrip, too. Use the Filmstrip to switch between open pictures as described in step 8.

Start It There
If you're at the Works Task Launcher, click **Picture It! Express** in the Programs list, and then click the **Start Picture It! Express Link.**

Other Picture Projects
You can use Picture It! Express to create photo albums, collages, cards, postcards, and more. Have fun with all the possibilities!

(5) If your picture is in a folder other than the default C:\My Documents\My Pictures\, use the drop-down list to select the proper disk and folder.

(6) Click the picture you want.

(7) Click **Open**.

(8) To switch to another picture, click it in the Filmstrip, and click **Switch To** in the Retriever window.

Editing Your Picture

Picture It! Express enables you to edit a picture by cropping it, flipping or rotating it, adding text, touching up defects, adding effects such as blurring and freehand painting, or applying a blurred edge. This task shows you how to work with a few of the image-editing possibilities in Picture It! Express.

Task 9: Adding an Effect

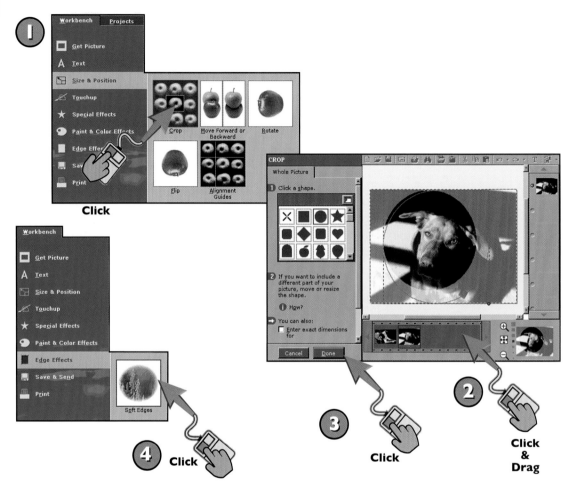

Click

Click

③ **Click**

② **Click & Drag**

④ **Click**

✓ **Pick a Picture**
Use the Filmstrip to select a picture for editing.

① Click **Size & Position** in the menu at the left side of the workbench, and click **Crop**.

② Click a crop shape, if desired, and then drag cutout handles to move and stretch the cropping zone.

③ Click **Done**.

④ Click **Edge Effects** in the menu at the left side of the workbench, and click **Soft Edges**.

Next Step

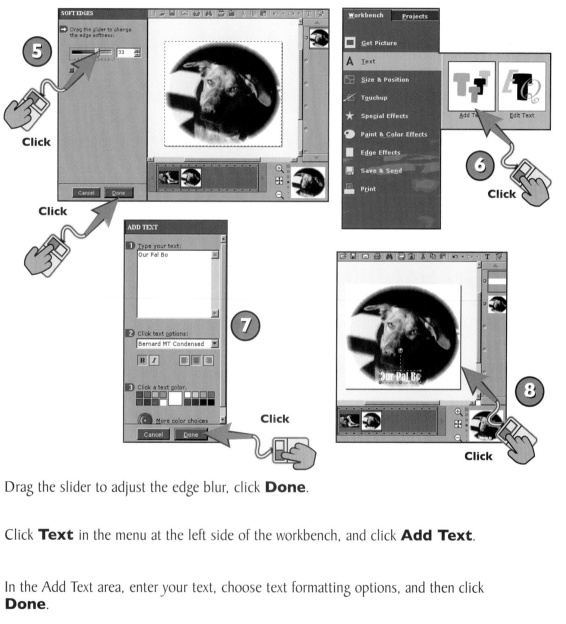

Correcting Your Photos

The Touchup choice on the Workbench enables you to correct problems with old photos that you've scanned in or have shot with a digital camera. You can adjust the brightness and contrast, fix the picture tint, remove the dreaded "red eye," and even eliminate scratches.

5 Drag the slider to adjust the edge blur, click **Done**.

6 Click **Text** in the menu at the left side of the workbench, and click **Add Text**.

7 In the Add Text area, enter your text, choose text formatting options, and then click **Done**.

8 Resize and reposition the text box as needed, and click outside the text box.

Task 10: Saving and Exiting

Completing the Picture

If you've scanned or created a new picture, you need to save it to store it on disk so you can use it in projects and documents you create. If you've edited an existing picture, you need to save your changes to it. This task shows you how to save, and then how to exit Picture It! Express when you complete your work.

✓ What Format?

If you're working with an existing picture that uses a format other than the Picture It! Express file format, you need to specify whether to save it as a Picture It! Express file, or save it in its original format. The advantage to saving it in the Picture It! Express format is that you can edit some of the effects that you might have applied, such as text effects.

Start Here

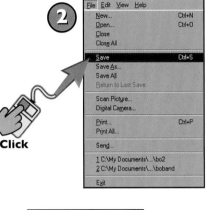

Click

Click

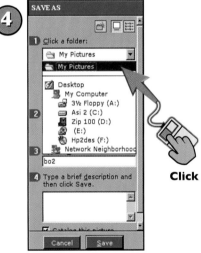

Click

Click

Click

① Use the Filmstrip to switch to the picture to save.

② Choose **File**, **Save**.

③ Click **Yes** if the Save in Picture It! Format? dialog box appears.

④ If needed, select the drive and folder to save to from the **Click a Folder** list.

Next Step

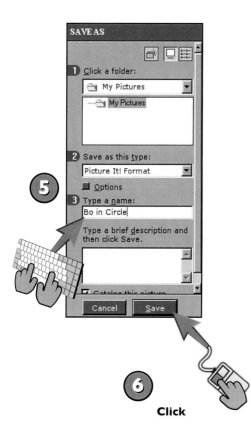

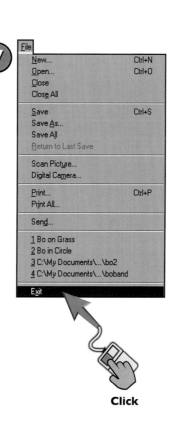

Click

Using Your Picture It! Pictures

After you've saved a file you've edited in either the Picture It! .mix file format or its original format, you can include the picture in your Home Publishing 2000 projects. Refer to Task 4 in this part to learn how to do so.

Click

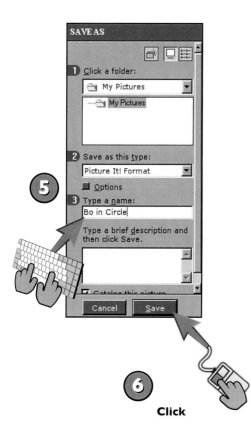 Edit the filename in the **Type a Name** text box.

Click **Save**.

Choose **File**, **Exit**.

ⓘ WARNING

You can switch between pictures in the Filmstrip without saving your work each time. So, be sure you save every picture, as needed, on the Filmstrip before exiting the program. Use the **File**, **Save All** command to save time. Right-click a picture in the Filmstrip, and click **Close** to close it.

Using the Reference Tools

Microsoft Works Suite 2000 also includes several other tools that can save you time. This last section covers the encyclopedia and street map programs. The Encarta 2000 encyclopedia can save you trips to the library and provides an interesting and entertaining introduction to a wide range of topics. Expedia Streets & Trips 2000 comes in handy when you need to plan a trip—either across town or across the country.

Tasks

Task 1: Starting Encarta Encyclopedia 2000

Launching the Encarta Encyclopedia

Even with all the access of the Web at your fingertips, don't view the Microsoft Encarta Encyclopedia 2000 as having inferior inform- ation. Depending on the topic you're searching for and the speed of your connection, Encarta might be much faster than searching the Web. If your kids use Encarta, they won't be running across adult material on the Web. And Encarta requires neither a phone line nor an Internet account, so there's no additional expense in using it.

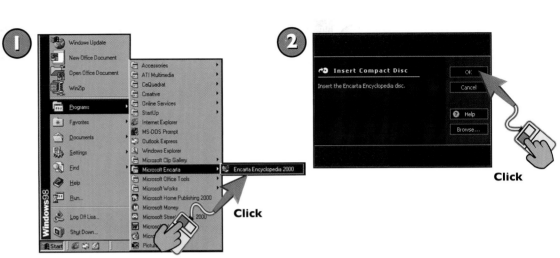

Click

Click

 Launch Time
You also can start Encarta from the Works Suite Task Launcher.

 Going Home
To return to the Home screen from another screen in Encarta, click **Home** on the menu bar.

1 Choose **Start**, **Programs**, **Microsoft Encarta**, **Encarta Encyclopedia 2000**.

2 When prompted, insert the Encarta CD-ROM (Disc 3 in the Works Suite set) into your CD-ROM drive and click **OK**.

3 Start working in Encarta. Leave the CD in until you've finished working with Encarta.

Task 2: Accessing Encarta Help

Start Here

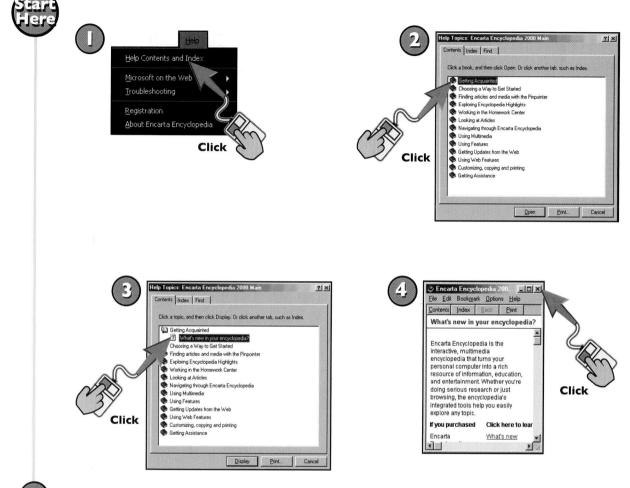

Click

Click

Click

Click

Getting Help in Encarta

Right off the bat, you can see that Encarta looks a little different from other Windows applications you've seen in this book. From the opening Encarta screen (called the Home screen), you can access a Help window and find out more about Encarta and how to use it to find information.

1. Choose **Help**, **Help Contents and Index**.

2. Double-click a book icon to see the topics it holds.

3. Double-click a topic icon to see its help.

4. After you review the help information, click the window **Close (X)** button to return to the Encarta Home screen.

✓ **Diving In**
If you want to take a look at some of Encarta's most interesting articles, click the **Encarta Explorer link** on the Home page. After the Explore screen appears, follow category links to articles.

Task 3: Finding an Article by Title

Searching for a Topic

Encarta organizes information alphabetically in articles. Each article title corresponds to an alphabetical entry in an encyclopedia volume. But instead of flipping through the pages of a bound volume to find the topic you want, in Encarta you type the article name.

✓ Using the Pinpointer

The Pinpointer dialog box enables you to specify the article title or other item to search for. Task 8 explains how to move it out of the way.

⚠ WARNING

After you use the technique of your choice to find articles and list them in the Pinpointer (as described in Tasks 3–7), click the **Reset Search** button to start again. Otherwise, your previous search technique remains active, and then the new search narrows the previous list of articles.

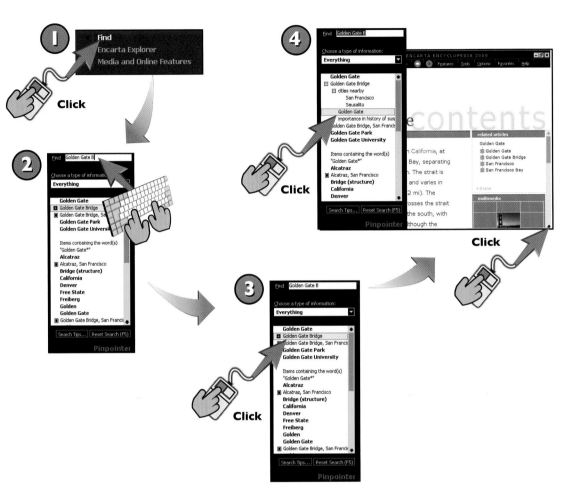

Start Here

Click

Click

Click

Click

1 Click the **Find** choice in the Home screen to display the Pinpointer.

2 Type the article title (or even part of it) to find in the Find text box at the top of the Pinpointer.

3 To view an article, click it in the list.

4 If the Pinpointer display additional choices, click the one you want. (Scroll to read more of the article.)

End Task

Task 4: Closing and Redisplaying the Pinpointer

Start
Here

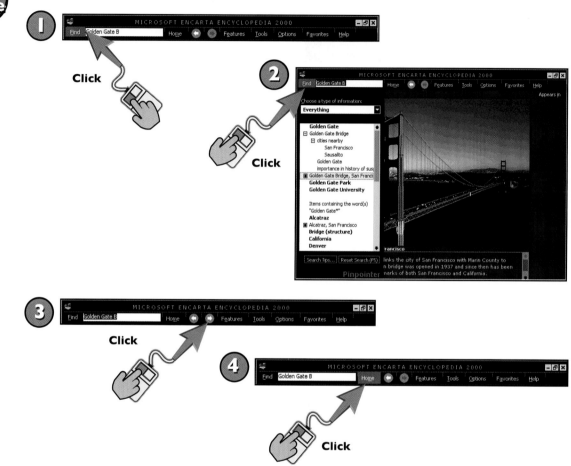

Click

Click

Click

Click

Viewing and Hiding the Pinpointer

When you select an article that you want to read, Encarta automatically puts away the Pinpointer so that the maximum amount of information can appear onscreen. When you're ready to search for another article, you redisplay the Pinpointer to do so, or you can back up from the Pinpointer and redisplay the previous article.

① With the Pinpointer closed, click **Find** on the Article screen menu bar to redisplay the Pinpointer.

② To minimize (hide) the Pinpointer, click **Find** again.

③ Click one of the arrow buttons on the menu bar to move between articles that you've displayed.

④ Click the **Home** button on the menu bar to move back to the Encarta Home screen at any time.

Task 5: Searching for a Word

Finding Articles That Contain a Certain Word

You can use the Pinpointer to search for information in a variety of ways. You are not limited to typing in a specific topic. The next four tasks in the book cover alternative ways to use the Pinpointer. This task begins by explaining how to search for information based on one word, two words, or even a question you enter.

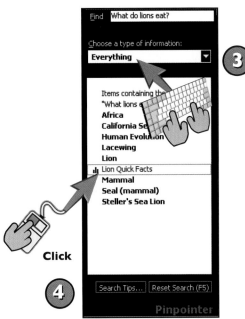

Click

Click

✅ **Reviewing the Results**
These alternative search techniques also enable you to find multiple articles and then to select the one that providing the information you need.

① Type a word or phrase in the Find text box on the Pinpointer.

② Click the article to view.

③ After redisplaying the Pinpointer, type your question in its Find text box.

④ Click the article to read.

Task 6: Finding an Article by Information Type

Start Here

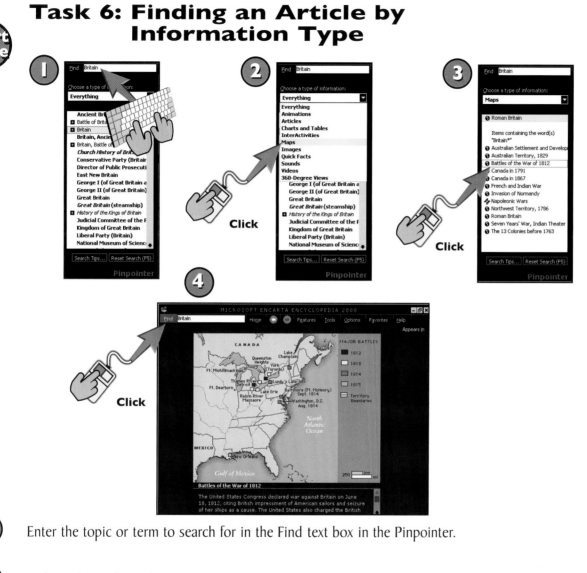

Click

Click

Click

Specifying an Information Type

In addition to organizing articles alphabetically, Encarta groups them by the type of information they hold—animations, charts and tables, maps, images, and so on. If you are interested in finding out more about something and want Encarta to list a particular type of information, use the **Choose a Type of Information** drop-down list in the Pinpointer.

---

1 Enter the topic or term to search for in the Find text box in the Pinpointer.

2 Make a choice from the Choose a Type of Information drop-down list.

3 Click the article you want to read in the list.

4 Click **Find** to redisplay the Pinpointer when you finish.

> ✓ **Resetting the Search**
> After you've displayed a list of categories in the Pinpointer, click the **Reset Search** button to choose another area of interest and its list of categories.

End Task

Task 7: Finding an Article by Time

Searching by Date

History students want to know when things happened, not just who did what and why. Encarta can help you find out more about events that happened and people who lived at about the same time.

Start Here

Click

Click

✓ How Date Searches Can Help

Searching for articles by time is a good way to select a subject for a school report. For example, say you know the Renaissance occurred around the year 1500. You can search for that date and scan through the listed articles for different Renaissance artists and scientists.

① Enter the year to search for in the Find text box in the Pinpointer.

② Click the article you want to read in the list.

③ Click **Find** to redisplay the Pinpointer when you finish.

End Task

Task 8: Finding an Article by Place

Start Here

Click

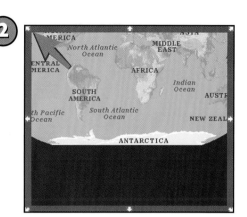

Click

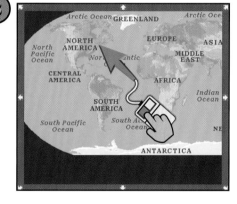

Click

Searching for Information About a Place

If you want to find out more about a region of the world, country, or city, you can find all the Encarta articles relating to it.

☑ **Going to a Region**
If you continue to click with the zoom pointer after you see the city names, new maps that have names of countries, regions, provinces, states, other political divisions, mountain ranges, bodies of water, and so on appear. You can click on many labels on any map when you see the paper and hand pointer, and then use the **Go to Article** choice. Not all labels have associated articles, though.

① Choose **Features**, **World Maps**.

② Point to an arrow to scroll the desired region into view.

③ Click with the zoom pointer as many times as needed on the map to see cities in the region. (It generally requires three or four links.)

④ Point to the name of a city of interest until you see the hand and paper pointer, click the city name, and click **Go To Article**.

Task 9: Viewing a Topic Within an Article

Reading an Article Topic

Just as you would divide up a lengthy report by adding headings and subheadings, Encarta divides its longer articles into more manageable topics. The outline on the left side of the Article screen lists the topics and subtopics within the current article. You can use that outline to navigate to different topics within the article.

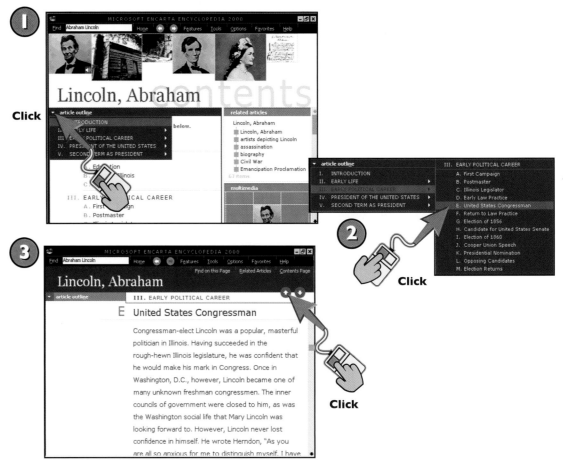

Start Here

Click

Click

Click

Click

① Click the drop-down arrow to the left of the Article Outline heading.

② Click a topic in the list to display it.

③ Review the specified topic onscreen, and use the up and down arrow buttons or the Article Outline menu to review other topics.

End Task

Task 10: Viewing an Animation

Start
Here

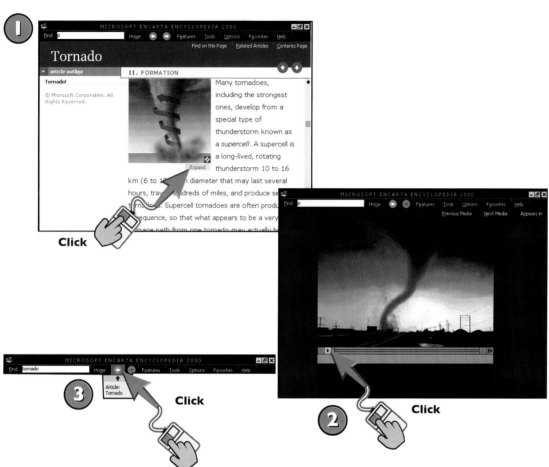

Opening an Article Movie

Some articles include animations or movie clips that you can play to see and hear more about the article topic. Animations (movies) appear as a picture with a small film strip icon in the lower-right corner. Here's how to play an animation.

(1) Click the picture for the animation or the small **Expand** button near its lower-right corner.

(2) Click the **Play** button to run the animation.

(3) Click the **Back** (left arrow) button on the menu bar to back up to the article.

✓ **Multimedia, Anyone?**
If you click in the Multimedia box in any article, Encarta displays a list of the photos, audio clips, maps, videos, charts, and illustrations about the topic. Click a choice in the Multimedia list to see or hear the specified item.

Task 11: Viewing a Graphic

Opening an Article Graphic

To save space onscreen so you can read more of an article, Encarta crops most of the pictures (graphic images) contained in articles. You can expand a picture to see more of it and the included caption, and then return it to its original size when you finish.

✓ **Graphic Printing or Copying**
After you expand a picture, you can right-click it, and then click **Print** or **Copy**. Click **Print** or **Copy** (respectively) in the dialog box that appears. Printing the image sends it directly to your printer. Copying it sends the image to the Windows Clipboard, from which you can paste it into another application file or document. The pasted image will have a credit line indicating the original photo source.

Start Here

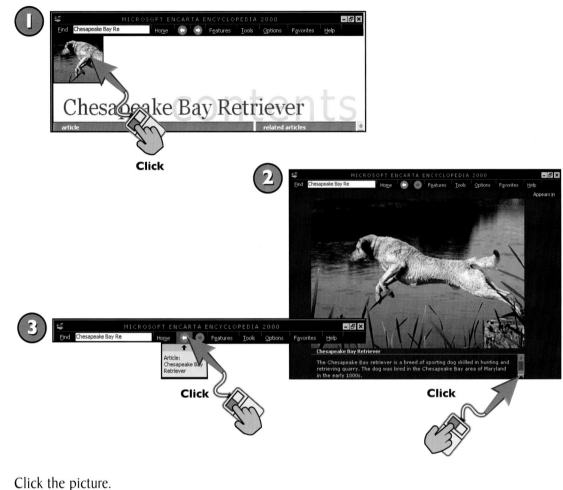

1 Click the picture.

2 Scroll the caption to view more of it, if you want.

3 Click the **Back** (left arrow) button on the menu bar to return to the article.

End Task

Task 12: Listening to an Audio Clip

Start Here

Playing a Sound from an Article

To make your learning experiences more enjoyable and memorable, some Encarta articles include sounds (audio clips) that you can play. After all, what's more clear, a description of a composer's music or a sample of it? A description of an animal's call or the call itself? Be on the lookout in your articles for pictures with sound icons in the lower-right corner. Play the sounds when you want to hear about as well as read about a topic.

✔ **Pinpoint**
You can select sounds, animations, graphics, and other elements directly from the Pinpointer list. Each different type of media is designated by a corresponding icon at the left. For example, sound items have a small speaker icon beside them.

1 Click the picture for the sound you want to play if you see it at the top of the article. (Otherwise, go to step 2.)

2 In the article, click the picture for the sound or the small **Expand** button near its lower-right corner.

3 Listen to the sound, which should play automatically. (If it doesn't, click the play button at the bottom of the picture for the clip.)

4 Click the **Back** (left arrow) button on the menu bar to back up to the article.

End Task

Task 13: Printing an Article

Making a Hard Copy

If you have more than one person clamoring to look up information in Encarta or want to read your information in a comfortable setting away from your computer, you can print it. In fact, you can print all or part of the article.

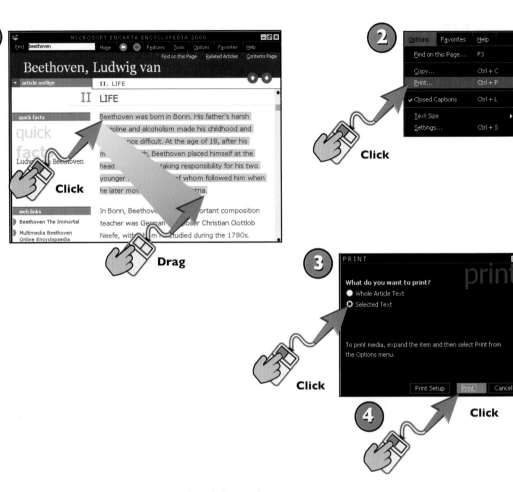

Start Here

Click

Drag

Click

Click

Click

1. Drag to select text to print in an article, if desired.

2. Choose **Options**, **Print**.

3. Click an option button to choose whether you want to print the **Whole Article Text** or the **Selected Text**.

4. Click the **Print** button to print.

End Task

Task 14: Exiting Encarta

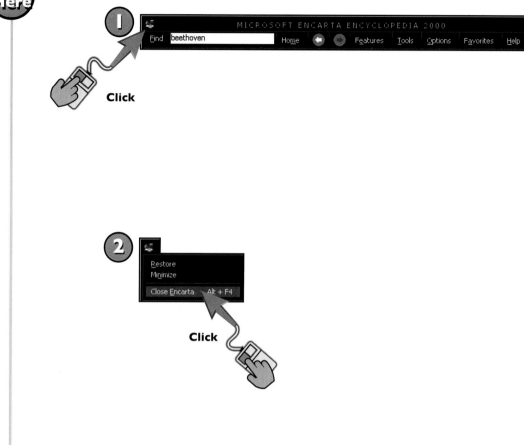

Click

Click

Closing Encarta

When you finish working with Encarta, you should exit the program to remove it from your computer's memory. Because Encarta relies on CD-ROM data, you also need to exit Encarta if you want to run another application that uses a CD-ROM or if you want to play an audio CD while you work. (Unless, of course, you have more than one CD-ROM drive on your system!)

① Open the **Control** menu for the Encarta application window.

② Click **Close Encarta**.

Launching Streets & Trips

When you get the travel bug, Works Suite can help you decide where to go, what to do, and how to get there. In this task, you learn to start up Expedia Streets & Trips 2000 and how to shut it down when you've finished working.

Task 15: Starting and Exiting Expedia Streets & Trips 2000

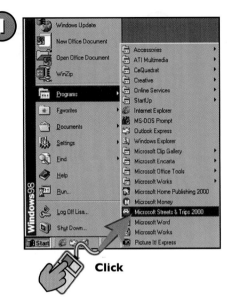

Click

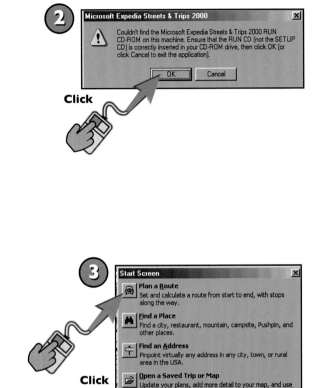

Click

✔ **Launch Time**
You also can start Expedia Streets & Trips from the Works Suite Task Launcher, or simply by inserting the run CD without using any command, as long as the AutoPlay feature works for your CD-ROM drive.

1 Choose **Start**, **Programs**, **Microsoft Streets & Trips 2000**.

2 When prompted, insert the Encarta CD-ROM (Disc 7 in the Works Suite set) into your CD-ROM drive and click **OK**.

3 Start working in Streets & Trips by clicking a choice or clicking **Close** on the Start Screen.

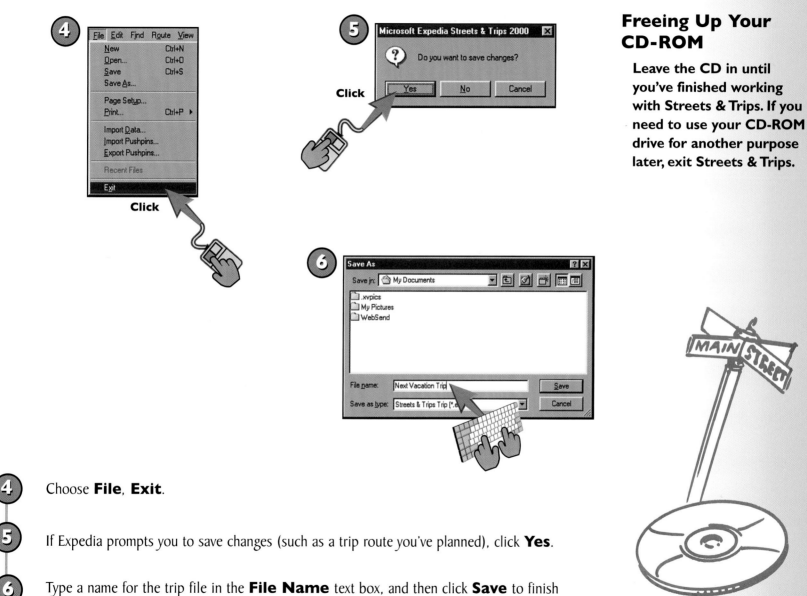

Freeing Up Your CD-ROM

Leave the CD in until you've finished working with Streets & Trips. If you need to use your CD-ROM drive for another purpose later, exit Streets & Trips.

(4) Choose **File**, **Exit**.

(5) If Expedia prompts you to save changes (such as a trip route you've planned), click **Yes**.

(6) Type a name for the trip file in the **File Name** text box, and then click **Save** to finish saving and closing.

Discovering Your Destination

If a family member is planning a move to another city, you might want to check out where he or she will be living. Or, if you yourself are searching for a new house or apartment, you might want to get an idea of where a potential new nesting place is located relative to your current home. You can use Streets & Trips to look up any address—whether in your town or another—and display it on a useful map.

Task 16: Finding an Address

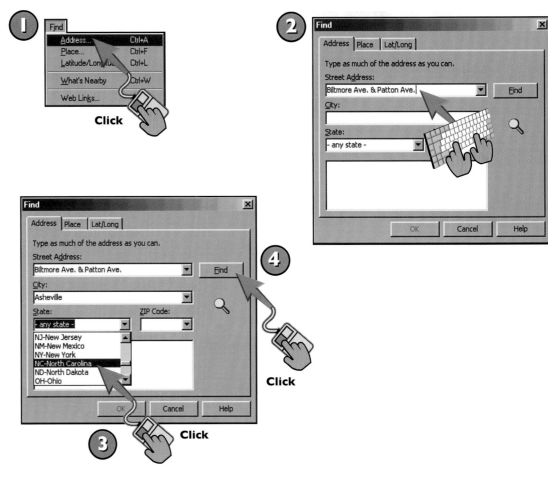

Click

Click

Click

✅ **Start Screen**
You also can start this process by clicking **Find an Address** in the Start Screen.

1. Choose **Find**, **Address**.

2. In the Street Address text box, enter either an actual address or an intersection in the format **Biltmore Ave. & Patton Ave.**.

3. Specify the **City**, **State**, and **ZIP Code** entries, or as many of them as you have.

4. Click **Find**.

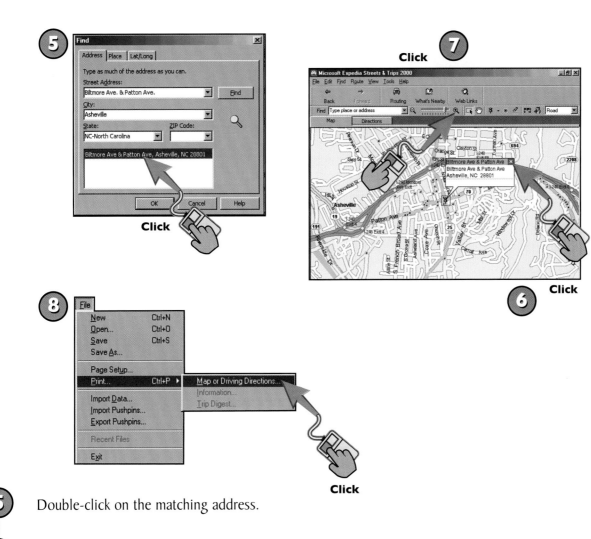

Click

Click

Click

Click

Click

Playing with Pushpins

When you find a major intersection as in the example shown in this task, the pushpin marking the intersection on the map might contain more information than just the street names. After you close the pushpin note, click the pushpin. The Select a Place dialog box that appears lists not only the intersection, but also restaurants and other significant attractions located at the intersection. Double-click one of them to see an icon for its location on the map. To redisplay the pushpin note, right-click the pushpin and click **Open**.

⑤   Double-click on the matching address.

⑥   Click the **Close** (**X**) button to close the pushpin note, if desired.

⑦   Use the **Zoom** buttons to zoom in or out.

⑧   Choose **File**, **Print**, **Map or Driving Directions**. Specify the desired print settings, and click **OK**.

End Task

Task 17: Planning a Travel Route

Getting There's All the Fun

Some spouses have little tiffs about how to get to another city or a specific location in your town. (Never happens to you, right?) To avoid these unfortunate incidents and ensure travel harmony, you can create and print driving directions using Streets & Trips.

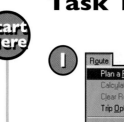

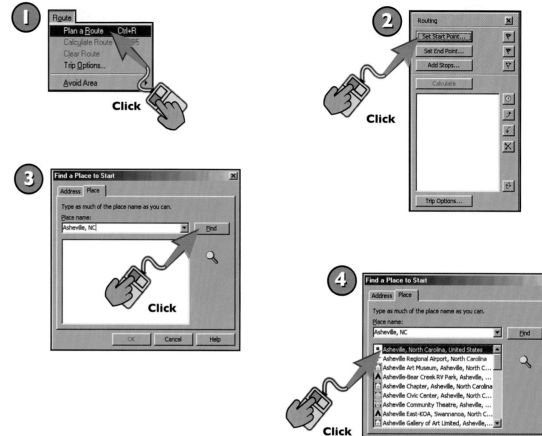

✓ **Start Screen**
You also can start this process by clicking **Plan a Route** in the Start Screen.

① Choose **Route**, **Plan a Route**.

② Click **Set Start Point**.

③ Make an entry in the Place Name text box, and then click **Find**.

④ Double-click on the location to use.

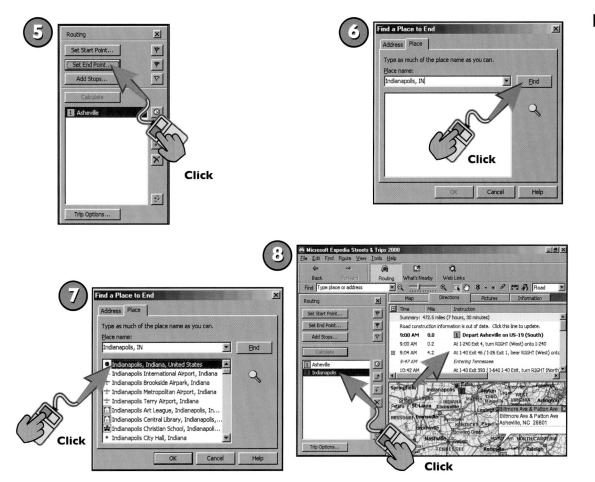

Planning Your Stops

You can use the **Add Stops** button in the Routing window to plan stops along your route. After you add a stop, a map for its location appears at the right side of the Streets & Trips window. You can **Zoom** in on the map to see icons indicating locations for restaurants, hotels, and attractions. Right-click an icon and click **Show Information** to see a specific address for a restaurant or hotel.

5 Click **Set End Point**.

6 Make an entry in the Place Name text box, and click **Find**.

7 Double-click the location to use.

8 Click **Calculate**, and review the instructions that appear on the right.

✓ **Directions In Print**
To print your finished directions, choose **File, Print, Map or Driving Directions.** Specify the desired print settings, and then click **OK**.

Setting Up Your Internet Connection

Internet Explorer 5.0 and Outlook Express 5.0 are part of Works Suite 2000, enabling you to surf the Web and use Internet e-mail and newsgroups. Windows includes the **Internet Connection Wizard** (**ICW**). You use the ICW to set up a Dial-Up Networking connection under Windows so that your modem can dial into your Internet account (via a phone line in your home) to connect with the Internet, enabling Internet Explorer and Outlook Express to work. The ICW walks you through the connection setup process, step by step.

You sign up for an Internet account with an Internet service provider (ISP). ISPs generally charge a flat monthly fee for Internet access. If you already have an Internet account, you do need to run the ICW to set up your system to dial the account. If you don't have an Internet account, you can use the ICW to connect to the Internet Referral Service's list of national ISPs with which you can obtain an account.

✓ Your Windows Version

This appendix illustrates ICW for Windows 98 Release 2. If you're using one of the Windows 95 releases or the first release of Windows 98, the ICW might look slightly different and have different steps. Just respond to the dialog boxes that your system's ICW presents, and you'll be successful in setting up your Internet connection. If you upgraded to Windows 98, the Setup program probably prompted you to set up your Internet connection, so you might not need to use this setup process. And, of course, if you've already set up your dial-up connection, there's no need to follow these steps.

The **Dial-Up Networking** connection (also called simply your Internet connection) that the ICW creates uses **TCP/IP** for connecting to the Internet. What you need to know about TCP/IP is that it connects you to your ISP in such a way that you can run Windows-based graphical software such as Internet Explorer and Outlook Express to work with the Internet by pointing and clicking.

⚠ WARNING

Some ISPs provide setup software to set up the Internet Connection for you so that you don't have to gather the information listed next. If you sign up with the Microsoft Network (MSN), for example, you'll use a different setup process. You need to use the ICW only if your ISP doesn't provide setup software or if you opt not to use the ISP's software. On the other hand, if there are glitches in the ISP's setup software and it doesn't quite work for you, try the ICW instead.

Before you run the ICW to set up the connection, gather these pieces of information from your Internet service provider:

- *ISP phone number.* This is the number you dial to connect.

- *Username, password, and e-mail address.* Your ISP provides these when you create your account. Note that your username might be a combination of letters and numbers rather than the name used for your e-mail address. For example, your username might be something like aa91562, but your e-mail address might be djones@earthlink.net.

- Domain and server information. You need to know the domain name for your ISP, which is usually something like `mindspring.com` or `earthlink.net`. You also need to know the online addresses for the servers (large online storage and routing areas) used for e-mail and newsgroups. E-mail usually requires two servers. The POP or POP3 server handles incoming mail and usually has an address such as `pop.mindspring.com`. The SMTP server handles outgoing mail and usually has an address such as `mail.mindspring.com`.

Follow these steps to use the ICW to establish your Internet connection:

I Click **Start**, point to **Programs**, and then to **Accessories**. On the Accessories menu, point to **Internet Tools** and click **Internet Connection Wizard**. Alternatively, you can double-click the **Connect to the Internet** icon on the desktop if you haven't previously used the Internet Connection Wizard; if you have, this icon launches Internet Explorer instead.

WARNING

If you're using a brand-new computer and try to start the ICW by double-clicking on the Internet Connection Wizard desktop shortcut or by double-clicking the Internet Explorer icon on the desktop, you might get a window prompting you to set up an MSN account. If this is the case, use the menu command described in step I to start the Internet Connection Wizard.

2 The first Internet Connection Wizard (ICW) dialog box appears. If you don't already have an account with an ISP, leave the first option button selected, click **Next**, and follow the rest of the wizard, which logs you on to the Microsoft Internet Referral Service, which you can use to sign up with an ISP. (After you sign up, the ICW should restart automatically. If it doesn't, restart these steps to use the ICW to set up your new connection, after the ISP provides the connection information you need.) If you already have an ISP account and want to download your account information, choose the second option button, which also logs you on to the Microsoft Internet Referral Service; from there you can select your ISP and have the account information downloaded. If you already have an account and want to set it up yourself, click the **I Want to Set Up My Internet Connection Manually**, **or I Want to Connect Through a Local Area Network (LAN)** option button (see the preceding figure), and then click **Next**. The rest of these steps assume you have an account with an ISP and clicked the third option button to set up the account manually.

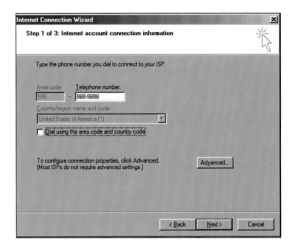

3 Assuming you're a home user and will be connecting to the Internet with a modem, leave **I Connect Through a Phone Line and a Modem** selected in the next ICW dialog box, and then click **Next**.

4 In the **Area Code** and **Telephone Number** text boxes, enter your ISP's phone number. Assuming your computer's dialing from the same area code, also click to clear the **Dial Using the Area Code and Country Code** check box. Click **Next**.

5 Enter your **User Name** and **Password**. Click **Next**.

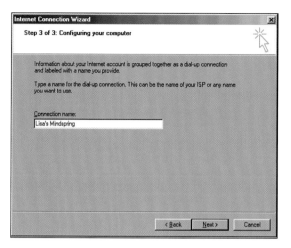

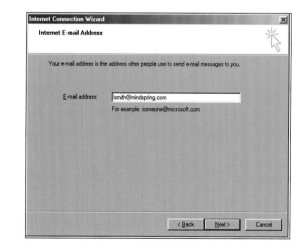

6 Enter a name to use for the Internet connection in the **Connection Name** text box. Click **Next**.

8 Enter the name or nickname you want to use for e-mail in the **Display Name** text box, and click **Next**.

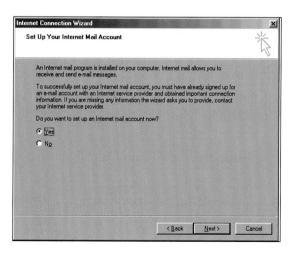

7 ICW asks whether you want to set up your Internet e-mail account. Leave **Yes** selected, and click **Next**.

9 Enter your e-mail address in the **E-Mail Address** text box. Click **Next**.

Appendix A

10 Enter the server addresses in the **Incoming Mail (POP3, IMAP or HTTP) Server** and **Outgoing Mail (SMTP) Server** text boxes. Click **Next**.

✅ **Your Incoming Mail Server**
If your ISP doesn't use a POP3 server, also select the correct server type from the My Incoming Mail Server Is a (Type) Server drop-down list in step 10.

11 Make or edit the **Account Name** and **Password** entries. Generally, the e-mail account name is different from the overall Internet account username, and consists of the part of your e-mail address that precedes the @ symbol. The mail password generally is the same as the overall account password. Leave **Remember Password** checked if you want to avoid having to type your password each time you send or receive mail, and check **Log On Using Secure Password Authentication (SPA)** if your ISP requires that method for mail retrieval.

12 Leave the check box near the center of the Internet Connection window checked, and click **Finish**.

13 In the Dial-Up Connection window, click **Connect** to dial and check your Internet connection. (If you check the **Connect Automatically** check box before connecting, you won't have to click the **Connect** button each time you start Internet Explorer or Outlook Express. It's up to you whether you prefer this feature or not.) After your system connects to the Internet, Internet Explorer 5.0 launches.

14 To close your Internet connection, use **File**, **Close** to exit the Internet Explorer software (or Outlook Express, if that's what you're using). In the Auto Disconnect dialog box, click the **Disconnect Now** button. To close the connection at any other time, right-click the connection icon in the system tray area at the right end of the taskbar, and click on **Disconnect**.

account   A Money 2000 account represents each savings, checking, or investment account you have in the real world. You use each Money account you create to hold the transactions for that account and to calculate the current account balance.

address bar   In a Web browser, this is the location where you type a URL (for a Web page) to display.

Address Book   A program that holds e-mail addresses and other information about your contacts for use in Outlook Express and other applications.

alignment   How text lines up relative to the document margin or cell border. Text can align to the left or right, or be centered between the margins or borders.

application window   Holds the application menus, buttons, the file or data you're working with, and other features.

appointment   In the Works Suite Calendar, represents an activity you've added to your schedule.

automatic page break   See *soft page break.*

browser   *See Web browser.*

browsing   Moving from Web page to Web page using browser software.

button   An onscreen icon (picture button) or area you click to perform a command or follow a link. Many of the Home Essentials applications offer a toolbar filled with buttons near the top of the application window.

Calendar   A Works Suite application that enables you to schedule your time and track birthdays and other events.

category   A label used in Money 2000 to identify an income or expense so that Money can report how you spend your money and where it comes from.

checking account   A Money 2000 account that corresponds to your real-world checking account. You can enter bills in the checking account and use Money to print checks to pay those bills.

classifications   Groupings of categories and subcategories and provide still further reporting effectiveness in Money.

clip art   Predrawn artwork you can insert in a document in Word 2000 or Home Publishing.

Clipboard   *See Office Clipboard.*

Clipboard toolbar   The toolbar that appears in Word 2000 when you cut or copy second and subsequent text selections and objects.

command   A menu choice that directs the application to perform a particular action, such as saving or printing a file.

contact   In the Address Book, a listing about one individual that includes information such as name, e-mail address, phone number, street address, and so on.

content identifier   The initial portion of an Internet address (URL), which identifies what kind of information the address holds and the protocol (communications method) used to exchange information with that address. The content identifier for Web addresses is `http://`.

context menu   *See shortcut menu.*

cut To remove the selected information from the file and place it in the Windows Clipboard. You can then paste this information to a new location in the document or even to another document or application.

database A program that enables you to store and organize lists of data, such as an address book list or home inventory.

Dial-Up Networking Windows' capability for connecting to and communicating with an online network via your modem. Windows enables you to create a Dial-Up Networking connection to dial into your Internet account.

document A letter, memo, report, or other text-based file created in a word processing program.

document window (file window) The window that holds an individual file within an application window.

download To transfer a file from the Internet or another computer to your computer via modem, so you can save it.

drag and drop To move or copy a selection by dragging it with the mouse and dropping it into place.

effect In Picture It! Express, a treatment you can apply to a picture, such as blurring or applying a soft edge.

e-mail software A program that enables you to send and receive messages over the Internet; Works Suite 2000 includes the Outlook Express 5.0 e-mail software.

field In a database program, one piece of information that appears in every entry (called a record), such as the *last name* for address entries. In a table or list view of a database, each field occupies a single column.

file A single document, spreadsheet, or database, named and stored on disk.

Financial Organizer Software (Financial Management Software) Software such as Money 2000, which tracks your bank and other investment accounts. These programs enable you to categorize income and expenses, print checks, and create budgets.

font The particular design of the characters in a selection. Each font has a name, such as Arial or Times New Roman. You select the font by name to apply it to a selection.

formatting Changes you make in the appearance of a selection or page. For example, you can make text bold or change the width of the margins (whitespace) around a page.

FTP (File Transfer Protocol) The communication method that your Web browser uses to download (transfer) a file from an Internet location to your computer.

hard page break A page break (new page start) that you insert where you want in a file, based on the file content and how you want it to look when printed.

highlighting See *selecting.*

home page Also called the start page. The first page your browser displays when you connect to the Internet. (Also the main or initial page for a Web site.)

hyperlinks See *links*.

Insert mode In Word, the mode where the word processor inserts text you type within existing text at the insertion point location. Existing text to the right of the insertion point moves right to accommodate the inserted text.

insertion point The flashing vertical hash mark that indicates where typed text will appear in a document or dialog box.

Internet The worldwide network of computers that stores and transfers information.

Internet account Dial-up Internet access that you purchase from an Internet service provider. When you obtain an account, you receive an account name and password you use to connect and log on via your modem. After you connect to your account (your Internet connection), you can use a browser to work on the Web, use your e-mail, and so on.

Internet Connection Wizard (ICW) A feature in Windows that leads you through the process of creating a Dial-Up Networking

connection so your modem can dial up and connect to your Internet connection.

Internet service provider (ISP) A company that sells Internet access. ISPs have large server computers with fast connections to the Internet. When you dial into your Internet account, your modem connects your computer to the ISP's server computer, which in turn connects your computer to the Internet.

links Specially formatted text, buttons, or graphics you click on a Web page to display (jump to) a different Web page.

location The second portion of an Internet address (URL), which identifies the server computer and directory storing the Web page that the address represents. For example, `www.mcp.com/que/` is an example of how the location portion reads.

manual page break See *hard page break*.

Maximize To expand a window so it fills the screen (for an application window) or the available space within the application window (for a file or document window).

Minimize To reduce a window to a button on the taskbar (for an application window) or icon within the application window (for a file window).

modem A device that enables your computer to communicate with another computer via telephone lines. (Newer types of modems enable your computer to communicate via special higher-speed phone lines, cable television connections, or even satellite.)

newsgroup A public discussion group on the Internet where participants can read and post messages. Each newsgroup centers around a particular topic.

Office Clipboard (Clipboard) A holding area in memory where your computer stores information you've cut or copied from a document. The Office Clipboard enhances the default Windows Clipboard, and can hold up to 12 selections.

Overtype mode In Word 2000, the mode where the word processor types over (replaces) text to the right of the insertion point location.

paragraph break   Pressing **Enter** to create a new paragraph in a word processing document.

paste   Inserting information from the Windows Clipboard into a file, at the location you specify.

Personalized menus and toolbars   In Word 2000, a feature that enables the program to add recently used commands to menus and recently used buttons to toolbars.

Places bar   In Word's Open and Save dialog box, this bar along the left side holds icons that you can use to quickly display folders and files that you work with frequently.

recognizing   How a spell checker identifies misspelled words. It compares the words in your file with a dictionary, passing by words it recognizes and stopping on words it doesn't.

record   In a database program, all the fields (individual pieces of information) for a single entry. For example, all the pieces of address information for one person would be a record.

recurring transaction   In Money 2000, a bill (check) or deposit (such as a pay deposit) that happens at regular intervals. You set up Money to remind you of a recurring transaction and enter the transaction information for you.

Redo   After you undo a correction, in some applications you can redo it if you change your mind.

Restore   Using a backup copy of a file to replace the current version if it becomes damaged.

scroll   Clicking a scrollbar to view a different area in a file or list.

search words   A word or phrase you enter in a Web search service to find Web pages covering the topic you entered.

selecting   Using the mouse or keyboard to place highlighting over text (or display handles around an object) so that the next command you perform applies to the selection.

shareware   Shareware is distributed via the honor system. If you install and use shareware, you should mail the specified modest payment to its author.

shortcut menu   A menu that appears when you right-click a selection, offering a concise list of commands you can perform on the selection.

soft page break   A page break inserted automatically in an application when you enter enough information to fill the current page.

spreadsheet   A file created in a spreadsheet program where you enter information in cells in a grid of rows and columns. You can then enter formulas (in other cells) to perform calculations.

Start Menu   The menu that appears when you click the Start button at the left end of the Windows taskbar. The Start menu enables you to access application startup commands, as well as startup commands for various Windows tools and applets.

start page   *See home page.*

Subcategory   A sublabel of a Money 2000 category, used to identify an expense or income transaction more precisely. *Also see category.*

TCP/IP   The language or protocol that your Dial-Up Networking connection uses to communicate with your ISP server computer and other computers on the Internet.

template   A file you can use to create a new document with predefined text and formatting. Most templates prompt you to fill in additional information and automatically format that information for you.

toolbar button   See *button.*

transaction   A bill (check), deposit, transfer, withdrawal, or cash machine action that you record in a Money 2000 account.

Undo   Reversing a command or action.

Uniform Resource Locator (URL)   The address for a particular file on the Internet, such as the address for a particular Web page. Also called an Internet address or Web address. The Web site name may begin with www, home, or nothing at all. Likewise, the site name may end with .com, .org, .net, or other extensions, as in

www.mindspring.com or www.circle.net. Similarly, the page name may end with a number of different extensions: .htm, .html, .asp, and so on. You must type the site name, directory, and page name exactly—including forward slashes, no spaces, correct capitalization, any special characters such as a hyphen or tilde (~), the correct site name, and correct page name and extension—or you'll get an error message.

view   A set of onscreen features in a program, such as particular screen elements and tools, user information, and zoom. You typically use the View menu to change views.

virus   A hidden program or file that travels along with files you download or copy to your computer. A virus hides on your system until it's triggered by a particular date and time or action, and then the virus runs. A virus might be benign, doing no more than displaying a message on your screen. Or, it might be malignant, destroying data or preventing your computer from working correctly. Use virus-checking software to identify and remove viruses.

Web (World Wide Web)   A subset of computers on the Internet that store information you can display graphically using a Web browser.

Web address   See *Uniform Resource Locator.*

Web browser   A program that enables your computer to display graphic information downloaded via modem from the World Wide Web.

Windows   The operating system that runs your computer. Its name stems from its method of displaying applications and files within movable and resizable windows (borders) onscreen.

wizard   A helper program that leads you through a process and prompts you to enter information to complete the task.

word processing program   A program you use to create and print text-based documents.

word wrap   Applied primarily in word processing programs, word wrap occurs when text reaches the right margin or border (filling the current line) so that the insertion point automatically moves to the next line.

WordArt In Word, used to apply a decorative effect such as 3D or curving to text you enter.

working offline In Internet Explorer 5.0 and Outlook Express 5.0, a feature that enables you to review information and create messages without being connected to the Internet.

Symbols-A

Index

C

File menu commands

G-H

Task Launcher (Works Suite)

U-V

W-Z